What People Are S

The Spirit of Freedom

Mark Russ's engaging and idiosyncratic blog has become a book, and it's a delight to revisit these pieces again. They cohere perfectly into a Quaker handbook that has as much to offer newcomers as it has to seasoned Friends. Original, insightful, and beautifully written, this book has all the hallmarks of an instant classic.

Geoffrey Durham, author of *What Do Quakers Believe?*, *Being a Quaker* and *The Spirit of the Quakers*

The Spirit of Freedom is a rich and stimulating book that expresses the best of the Quaker spirit: a listening spirit, open to difference and to change. In this book Mark Russ offers an extraordinarily wide-ranging exploration of key Quaker, Christian and human concepts. He brings fresh, and refreshing, insights to some of the much-loved Quaker *Advices and Queries* and talks of the need to ask better questions; of God as relationship; of the different kinds of silence; of evil. Wearing his learning lightly, Mark uses Biblical and historical references, but the strength of the book is its reliance on his own experience and insights. His very personal approach, as a gay Christian Quaker, invites and challenges each of us as unique human beings to allow the Light to shine on our own failings, find our own ministry, and express it in our worship and daily life.

Jennifer Kavanagh, author of *Practical Mystics*, *The World is our Cloister*, *A Little Book of Unknowing* etc.

In *The Spirit of Freedom* Mark Russ invites readers on a profound theological journey that blends Quaker wisdom with a modern and diverse perspective. His insightful essays, collected from years of thoughtful blogging, explore the essence of Quakerism rooted in Christianity, drawing inspiration from the life and teachings of Jesus. Through engaging reflections, Mark challenges and inspires readers to embrace love in action, obedience to God, and a deeper understanding of our Quaker heritage. This remarkable work promises to enrich the Quaker community and beyond.

Peterson Toscano, Queer, Quaker Bible Scholar, Activist, and host of *Quakers Today* podcast

"What helps nourish us as a people of the Light? What helps us bear witness to the reign of the Spirit of Freedom?" In this fascinating book, Mark Russ offers us insightful explorations into Quaker theological ideas. He tenderly unpicks much-quoted Quaker writings and 'beliefs', nudging us to take them further. Is our understanding as clear as it could be? Is there more that could help us on our spiritual way? Here is an inspiring must-read for all those who want to delve into what it means to be a Quaker today and it is sure to prompt many challenging, deep and enjoyable discussions, both between individuals and within the self. In this process we can "...become aware of God ... to find our rightful place in the cosmos, allowing ourselves to be led further and further into Love."

Joanna Godfrey Wood, author of *Travelling in the Light*, *In STEP with Testimony*, *In Search of Stillness*, and *In Search of Hope*

The Spirit of Freedom is an exciting collection of "unsystematic theology," perfect for daily readings, weekly devotional reflections, or joyful group discussion. With this complimentary volume to his superb *Quaker-shaped Christianity*, Mark has enacted a great service to those wishing to explore or to deepen their Quaker faith.

Ben Pink Dandelion, Professor of Quaker Studies at the University of Birmingham, author of *Open for Transformation*

Mark Russ is an authentic Quaker teacher and prophet. He reveals the best of our religious tradition, reshaped by the collision with the urgent challenges of our times. This is a book to be meditated on and wrestled with. Thoughtful, moving and provocative, *The Spirit of Freedom* presents a radical, inclusive vision of the Christian Quaker Way.

Craig Barnett, author of *The Guided Life*

In this fascinating little book, Mark Russ models a way of doing Quaker-shaped Christian theology that succeeds in being both scholarly and accessible. Whether unpacking the theology implicit within *Advices and Queries*, gently challenging Friends about their ways, or grappling with issues of oppression and liberation, he demonstrates that thinking theologically about such matters can help rather than hinder us in acting with justice and compassion.

Stuart Masters, Programme Coordinator (History and Theology) at Woodbrooke, and author of *The Rule of Christ: Themes in the Theology of James Nayler*

The Spirit of Freedom

Previous Titles

Quaker Shaped Christianity: How the Jesus story and the Quaker way fit together, Christian Alternative Books, 9781803410548

The Spirit of Freedom

Quaker-shaped Christian Theology

Mark Russ

CHRISTIAN ALTERNATIVE
BOOKS

London, UK
Washington, DC, USA

CollectiveInk

First published by Christian Alternative Books, 2024
Christian Alternative Books is an imprint of Collective Ink Ltd.,
Unit 11, Shepperton House, 89 Shepperton Road, London, N1 3DF
office@collectiveinkbooks.com
www.collectiveinkbooks.com
www.christian-alternative.com

For distributor details and how to order please visit the 'Ordering' section on our website.

Text copyright: Mark Russ 2023

ISBN: 978 1 80341 663 2
978 1 80341 672 4 (ebook)
Library of Congress Control Number: 2023945575

A CIP catalogue record for this book is available from the British Library.

Design: Lapiz Digital Services

UK: Printed and bound by CPI Group (UK) Ltd, Croydon, CR0 4YY
Printed in North America by CPI GPS partners

We operate a distinctive and ethical publishing philosophy in
all areas of our business, from our global network of authors to
production and worldwide distribution.

Now the Lord is the Spirit, and where the Spirit of the Lord is, there is freedom. **2 Corinthians 3.17**

Contents

Preface

In 2013 I began publishing my theological reflections on a blog called jollyquaker.com. The name comes from the book, *A Testament of Devotion* by the twentieth-century Quaker mystic Thomas Kelly. Kelly writes "I'd rather be jolly Saint Francis singing his canticle to the sun, than a dour sobersides Quaker."[1] Not wanting to make a choice between jollity and Quakerism, I chose to be a jolly Quaker. When I created the blog, I was teaching music in primary schools in East London. A decade later I have spent seven years as a tutor for the Woodbrooke Quaker Study Centre in Birmingham, England, published my first book *Quaker Shaped Christianity* (2022), and am now in the early stages of PhD study. With a decades' worth of blog posts under my belt, I decided it was time to collect the best of my writing into a book, this book in fact.

The essays in this collection are grouped according to theme, rather than the date they were originally written, and all of them have been updated and in some cases partially rewritten. A couple of introductory chapters explain what I think it means to "do" theology. The chapters in "Part 1: Speaking of God" address speaking of, speaking to, knowing, and listening to God. "Part 2: Worshipping God" deals with the nature of Quaker worship, and how Quakers do it and prepare for it. "Part 3: Being God's witnesses" reflects on the various challenges of living faithfully in a broken web of relationships, both within and without the Quaker community.

I need to clarify who I mean by "the Quaker community." Since its beginnings in seventeenth-century England, Quakerism has spread across the globe and taken various forms. When I speak of "Quakers" I'm specifically referring to Quakers in Britain and the kind of Quakerism they practice, which is often spoken of as "liberal" Quakerism. I also use the term

"Friends," which is how Quakers often refer to themselves. One of the characteristics of liberal Quakerism today is theological diversity. Perhaps surprisingly, I make no attempt to reflect this diversity in this book. Everyone who does theology does so from their own context. The theology I do is from a specifically Christian perspective. It's the only place I can speak from, and I know that Quakers, both Christian and non-Christian, appreciate this clarity of focus even if they don't always agree with me. I hope that Quakers in other parts of the world and from other theological backgrounds might find what I have to offer useful too.

Although I've organized the various essays so they can be read consecutively, giving the book a particular shape, they were not originally written in such a systematic way. "Systematic" is a label given by academic theologians to the kind of theology seeking to fit all the pieces of the theological jigsaw puzzle into a neat and tidy pattern. A few theologians have had the time and resources to create colossal multi-volume works exploring as many aspects of Christian theology as possible, some dying before they were able to finish the task. However, most theology is highly unsystematic. People do theology in response to specific situations. This is particularly true of Quakers, who in their early days were printing pamphlets left, right, and center responding to their various critics. Each chapter in this book was written in response to a question or annoyance I was wrestling with at a particular time. For a more methodical explanation of my theology, I direct readers to my first book, *Quaker Shaped Christianity*. At one point, I *did* attempt a systematic approach to Quaker theology, teasing out the theological underpinnings of the *Advices and Queries*. These are 42 pithy statements that capture the core of the Quaker faith in Britain. They appear as the first chapter of *Quaker Faith and Practice*, the authoritative collection of Quaker writings also known as the "book of discipline" used by Quakers in Britain. They're also published in a slim red booklet all by themselves. The brevity of each statement belies the layers of wisdom they contain. I wrote reflections on the first twelve before circumstances returned me to my more unsystematic approach.

In effect, this is a book that has taken me a decade to write. My writing style has developed alongside my own growth in life and in Spirit, and so there are variations in tone from chapter to chapter. My reflections on the *Advices and Queries* have the forthright sound of vocal ministry, the words spoken during Quaker worship. This reflects the spiritual power of the *Advices* and the role they play in the life of the Quaker community. Other chapters have a much more conversational tone. I've chosen not to iron out these stylistic creases, leaving them as a testament to my unsystematic theology. It has been interesting to notice the influence of particular voices, such as those of Thomas Kelly and C.S. Lewis, that come up again and again in the earlier essays. As much as I still love these authors, my reliance on dead White men represents a deficit in my theological education, one I promise to correct in future books. My theology has changed and will continue to do so. I believe everything in this book is worth putting into print, but it doesn't represent the end point of my theologizing. My intention in placing "Quaker theology and Whiteness" as the final chapter is to point toward the next stage of my theological work. It was written at the beginning of my interest in Quakerism and racism, a subject I'm now researching as a PhD student.

One particular change I've made throughout the book is substituting the phrase "Kingdom of God" for "kin-dom of God." This concept of the kin-dom of God was first given prominence by Ada María Isasi-Díaz in her book *Mujerista Theology: A Theology for the 21st Century* (Orbis Books, 1996). For most of my faith journey, I have been comfortable with terms like "Kingdom" and "Lord," knowing that in their first-century context, these were radical political terms. To say "Christ is

Lord" is to say that Caesar isn't, and to announce the arrival of God's reign is a challenge to the empire of Rome. However, even with this caveat, the hierarchical and patriarchal nature of these terms is a stumbling block today. The phrase "Kingdom of God" no longer feels politically subversive. Isasi-Díaz's concept of "kin-dom" keeps the communal vision of God's promised future without the baggage that "Kingdom" has accumulated.

All biblical quotes, unless otherwise stated, are from the New Revised Standard Version. Whenever I first mention a particular book of the Bible in a chapter, I give its full name (for example, 1 Corinthians). Further mentions are then abbreviated in a conventional way (1. Cor.). When I write of the Hebrew Bible, I'm referring to what some readers may call the Old Testament. When quoting from *Quaker Faith & Practice*, the "book of discipline" used by Quakers in Britain at the time of writing and first published in 1994, I indicate paragraphs by the abbreviation "Qf&p" followed by the paragraph number. I also occasionally refer to *the Friend* which is a weekly British Quaker periodical.

The decade of writing represented by this book is unimaginable without the encouragement of my friends, fellow authors, and readers. This book is dedicated to everyone who has taken the time to read my work and get in touch with supportive comments. I'm particularly grateful to the wonderful people who joined me for a book group in January 2023, reading and discussing *Quaker Shaped Christianity* over six weeks. Their enthusiastic engagement gave me the confidence to put this new book together. Special thanks go to Craig Barnett who, many years ago, told me my blog deserved to become a book; to Joanna Godfrey Wood for proofreading the first draft of this book and giving invaluable feedback on many of the chapters; and to Jennifer Kavanagh for telling me repeatedly to submit a manuscript to Christian Alternative Books, because she knew I had something to say.

Paul's words on the Spirit of Freedom in 2 Corinthians 3.17 continue to inspire me and provide the title and epigram of the book. I have experienced this Spirit and continue to discover new depths to what God's freedom means. My final thanks must always be to the God of my life, Creator, Lover, and Protector, whom I can never thank enough.

Introduction

Doing Quaker Theology

Chapter 1

The Quaker Gospel

Take heed, dear Friends, to the promptings of love and truth in your hearts. Trust them as the leadings of God whose Light shows us our darkness and brings us to new life. **Advices and Queries 1**

"What do Quakers believe?" A Quaker might hesitate to answer this question, fearing they'll come across as pushy. They might more comfortably answer with what Quakers don't believe, or talk about sitting in silence, which to the enquirer might be construed as another negative: sitting doing nothing. A better answer might be found in the opening words of the *Advices and Queries*, the pithy collection of wisdom that attempts to capture the depth and breadth of Quaker wisdom in 42 paragraphs.

Here we find the "good news" of the Quakers. Here there is no hesitancy. This is not a suggestion, it's an exhortation. Take heed. Listen. Trust.

Between the lines of these two sentences, an expansive story can be read. The language of listening and leading speaks of a relationship. This is not a relationship of equals but between one who leads and one who listens. This is a relationship between God and humanity.

Why are we being asked to trust these leadings? Because this relationship has broken down. Both hearing and trusting the leadings of God must be difficult if we need such a reminder. Why has this relationship broken down? Why is it difficult? Because we are in a place of darkness, a darkness that is in opposition to the newness of life. It seems we can't emerge from this darkness by our own efforts. We can't even see the darkness without help. We need Light with a capital "L," and this Light belongs to God.

What else does this say about God? This is a God that communicates with us, and this communication occurs inwardly. These promptings, God's leadings, occur in our hearts, in our inner, emotional life. These promptings are of love and truth, corresponding to the traditional twin characteristics of the Christian God: mercy and justice. God both comforts and discomforts, soothes and reproaches, embraces and unveils.

This is a God who calls us and, if we respond, reveals the darkness we inhabit, the darkness that inhabits us, and will lead us out of it to new life. For all that "being saved" is absent from liberal Quaker vocabulary, here we have a story of salvation, of a saving relationship.

Here we have a description of a fractured human condition where we are ignorant of our own ignorance, and the promise of a restored relationship with a saving God who both reveals and casts out darkness.

Importantly, this is not an individualistic statement. It's communal. "Take heed, dear Friends." It speaks of our hearts and our darkness. This is a relationship with God that takes place in community. We are called to listen together, to trust and be led together, to be judged together, and healed together.

For two sentences, this is explosive stuff.

Chapter 2

Theology as Ministry

The previous chapter is an example of Quaker theology, words about the religious life from a Quaker perspective. I read, think, and write about my Quaker beliefs and practices and so I call myself a Quaker theologian. You may be surprised to hear "Quaker" and "theologian" in the same sentence. Theology is a word liberal Quakers aren't universally comfortable with. I've heard Friends say "we don't need theology" and "it doesn't matter what we believe, it's how we live that counts." In Quaker spaces, it's not unusual to hear theology characterized as un-spiritual, stale, closed, divisive, and impractical. This Quaker anti-theology attitude has a long history. The first Quakers in the seventeenth century saw theological debate as a distraction from real spiritual experience, and the product of power-hungry Church councils. They experienced theological argument as a tool of oppression leading people into unbelief.[2] They saw theology as "soaring, airy head-knowledge" playing no role in salvation.

Yet despite this suspicion of theology, from the beginning Quakers have always needed to theologize, to describe and explain their faith to themselves and others. Early Friends produced an abundance of undeniably theological writings. The phrase "airy head-knowledge" comes from Robert Barclay's *Apology*, written in 1678 and one of the first substantial theological arguments for the Quaker faith. *Quaker Faith & Practice*, the contemporary "book of discipline" used by Quakers in Britain, is brimming with theology. Where theology is concerned, Quakers find themselves pulled in two directions. We shy away from the idea of theology, yet we can't stop ourselves from doing it.

To Quakers who see theology as a stumbling block or necessary evil, I have two thoughts to offer. First, theology isn't confined to academia. It's a very ordinary activity and we do it all the time. We can't escape it. When we attempt to make sense of the Divine and our relationship to it, we're doing theology. "It doesn't matter what we believe" is itself a theological statement. We've fallen into a trap of thinking we must choose between "theology" and "no theology," but "no theology" isn't an option for a religious community. The real choice is between good and bad theology. Does our God-talk help us to flourish, or does it diminish us? There's a lot of harmful, even deadly theology out there, and I can understand why some might want to be rid of it altogether, but bad theology needs to be met by better theology. As long as we're Quakers we can't opt out.

Second, theology is my ministry. Since theology is something we all do, it's useful to have people who can help us do it better. I feel called to be one of those people. Doing theology is how I serve my Quaker community. There's a passage in *Quaker Faith & Practice* that describes my ministry perfectly:

There is also the ministry of teaching which combines "the potency of prayer and thought." It recalls the meeting to the discoveries of truth, the perception of the acts of God in the lives of individuals. It includes the effort to understand and to interpret the central fact of Jesus Christ and his place in history, and the searchings and findings of men and women down the ages and in our own day as they have sought to relate new discoveries and insights to their understandings of eternal truth. (Qf&p 2.67)

Quakers sometimes pit the intellect against spirituality, as if thinking about things is a hurdle to spiritual growth. In my experience, this isn't the case. For me, theology is a response to encountering God. In my late teens, I began to have what I can only describe as ecstatic spiritual experiences, where I was left in awe of the Divine. I then needed to make sense of these experiences. I needed to do theology. A classic definition of theology given by Anselm of Canterbury in the eleventh century is "faith seeking understanding." You could say, and many have, that God-talk begins with grateful amazement. Then in seeking to understand I'm led back to faith. In doing God-talk I return to praising God. C. S. Lewis wrote "I believe that many who find that 'nothing happens' when they sit down, or kneel down, to a book of devotion, would find that the heart sings unbidden while they are working their way through a tough bit of theology with a pipe in their teeth and a pencil in their hand."[3] This has often happened to me but without the pipe. Theology is both a response to the God who is the Spirit of Life and a way to that same Spirit.

Theology can also be thought of as dry and dusty, pitting intellect against imagination. In my experience, good theology can be imaginative, playful, and creative. Theology can be beautiful. Films, music, theatre, and graphic novels can be intensely theological. The role of the imagination is crucial to doing life-enhancing theology. In the Bible, Divine Wisdom is portrayed as playfully delighting and rejoicing in creation (Proverbs 8.30-31). Quakers sometimes characterize theology as being about certainty, in opposition to the Quaker preference for uncertainty and being "open to new light," but I'm convinced openness is a feature of good theology. Theology is about exploring a constantly expanding landscape. The journey is full of new discoveries and the vistas get larger and larger, but I never get any closer to the horizon. Since I believe God is infinite, this is just the sort of journey I should expect.[4] I can never get to the end of God, but I'm not uncertain about everything. There are things I'm sure about, that I have a firm confidence in, such as the love of God, but that doesn't close me off to new insights. I don't have to choose between uncertainty and certainty. I can have a mix of both. Theology is about learning to ask better questions and getting a better knowledge of what I don't know.

The early Quaker suspicion of theology was fueled by religious conflict, specifically between Christians. Violent disagreements over theological issues like baptism work against the peace and unity Christians are meant to enjoy. But this doesn't mean theology can be set aside. We need to make a theological commitment to respectful dialogue, seeking the wellbeing of all people. Respectful dialogue isn't just a means to an end. It's meaningful in itself as an expression of a loving relationship. Everything that works for peace and the liberation of all things, including respectful dialogue and mutual understanding, is work for God's kin-dom.

Quakers can pit theology against practice, right belief (orthodoxy) against right action (orthopraxy), as if theology is inherently abstract and unrelated to "real life." But why do we need to make those distinctions? Our behavior is surely influenced by our beliefs. We demonstrate our beliefs through our behavior. Right belief and right action go together. Good theology is public, political, and practical, inextricable from human relationships and power struggles. Good theology can help us understand what it means to be faithful in a world of gross inequality, climate chaos, and the possibility of nuclear apocalypse. Quaker-shaped Christian theology can never be purely about the inner mental or spiritual life of the individual. Good theology gives us hope in today's world.

Theology is my ministry. I find it a life-enhancing activity, through which I respond to and experience the Spirit of Love. I give thanks for Quakers who value and encourage their theologians. It can sometimes feel like a lonely occupation. I hope this support and encouragement can become an increasingly mainstream Quaker value, where Friends foster both ordinary theology in their Quaker communities and nurture those individuals who have a calling to a deeper engagement with theological thought.

Part 1

Speaking of God

Chapter 3

Our Experience of God Is Not God

Bring the whole of your life under the ordering of the spirit of Christ. Are you open to the healing power of God's love? Cherish that of God within you, so that this love may grow in you and guide you. Let your worship and your daily life enrich each other. Treasure your experience of God, however it comes to you. Remember that Christianity is not a notion but a way. **Advices and Queries 2**

The first *Advices and Queries* addresses the community of "dear Friends." Now we focus on the individual. There is much to unpack in this beautiful and seemingly simple paragraph.

First, we must ask what the "spirit of Christ" is. In the Bible "spirit" is synonymous with breath and the wind. Spirit invisibly animates and enlivens. The Spirit of "Christ" is the vibrant Life we see in Jesus of Nazareth. In John 20.22 the resurrected Jesus breathes on his disciples, saying "receive the Holy Spirit." This is the Spirit of Freedom (2 Corinthians 3.17). This Spirit of Christ is mysteriously available to us all and is one of order. We are invited to allow this spirit, which is also the love of God, to bring healing and order to our broken and chaotic lives. God won't do this without our permission. Christ stands at the door and knocks (Revelation 3.20). We must open the door before this work can begin.

What is "that of God within"? God can't be broken into pieces. We don't have a fragment of God inside us. Neither do we have one of many "gods" within us. Is "that of God" a natural capacity to respond to God? I don't think so. The first *Advices and Queries* suggests that our capacity to hear and obey

11

God has been impaired. "That of God" in the traditional Quaker understanding is a seed God plants in our hearts. It lies dormant in the earth, waiting for the Light to awaken it. We must cherish it, treasure it, and care for it, allowing the seed to grow within us. The process of our healing requires work. The garden of our inner life needs careful tending.

The message is a holistic one. We are asked to bring the whole of our lives to God. We cannot have a "religious" or "spiritual" life separate from our "work" or "love" life. Our worship and our daily life are intimately linked. If we attempt to keep them separate, we stifle the seed of God. The God-seed needs to flourish and bloom in every aspect of our being and life. Like the mustard seed, it's an invasive plant that will grow to tremendous proportions if we allow it.

We are asked to treasure our experience of God. An important point must be made here: our experience of God is not God. Our experiences of God will vary, but the variation is in our experience rather than God's-self. God remains the same, ever mysterious and "other," inwardly knowable yet still paradoxically hidden through the Spirit of Christ. It's misleading to speak as if Quakerism is based on "pure experience" with an accompanying rejection of "talk about experience." There is no such thing as pure, unmediated experience. Our experience of God is not God. Our experience of God is vital in all senses of the word, and so are the ways we communicate with each other about these experiences. This brings me to the continually misused word "notion."

What is a notion? I have heard this word used to dismiss any idea, or even theology and language altogether. I have heard similar mistreatments of Paul's words that "the letter kills" (2 Cor. 3.6). This is not helpful. Ideas, concepts, and theories allow us to communicate with one another. If all ideas are notions, then so are phrases like "Christianity is not a notion but a way." Rather, a notion is an idea empty of Divine Truth and is treated as an end in itself. Our ideas and theories are important, indispensable tools useful only when we use them as such. As soon as we mistake them for what they point towards they lose their usefulness and become notions. God is always bigger than our ideas of God.

Christianity is not a notion but a way. Christianity (originally referred to as "the Way" in, for example, Acts 9.2) is not an intellectual curiosity but a story. It's a vision promising the transformation and purification of the entire cosmos in the fires of Divine Love. It's a community to be joined, not an idea to be entertained. It's not a marker of social respectability or an insurance policy but a glorious adventure bearing the marks of crucifixion. Commitment to Quakerism is not a commitment to a purely abstract theology or a practice without a theory. It's a commitment both to an embodied theology and a storied practice. Quakerism is a lived tradition.

Chapter 4

What Is "That of God in Everyone"?

"That of God in everyone" is a theological cornerstone of Quakerism in Britain today, but what does it mean? In this chapter, I explore how the meaning of this phrase has changed since the first days of Quakerism, and what I think it means by way of theologian Jürgen Moltmann and the idea of God's "Shekinah."

"That of God in everyone" originally comes from a letter from early Quaker leader George Fox to other Quaker ministers, written down by Ann Downer whilst Fox was imprisoned in Cornwall in 1656:

> ...And this is the word of the Lord God to you all, and a charge to you all in the presence of the living God: be patterns, be examples in all countries, places, islands, nations, wherever you come, that your carriage and life may preach among all sorts of people, and to them; then you will come to walk cheerfully over the world, answering that of God in every one. (Qf&p 19.32)

Even though these words come from the seventeenth century, they didn't become a well-known Quaker phrase until they were popularized by Quaker author Rufus Jones at the beginning of the twentieth century.[5] "That of God in everyone" is now an established part of Quaker vocabulary. Today I see Friends use it as a basis for the Quaker understanding of equality and as a springboard for work on diversity and inclusion. We are all of equal worth because we all have "that of God" in us. It's also used to emphasize the universalist character of Quakerism.

Everyone's spiritual experience is worth learning from because we all have our own experience of "that of God." Because it's something we all have and confers equal worth on us all, it's used interchangeably with the idea of the "Inner Light."

Early Friends held a different understanding of the "Inner Light." They spoke of the "inward Light," and it wasn't naturally a part of us. In his *An Introduction to Quakerism* (2007) Ben Pink Dandelion describes this "inward Light" as something coming from outside, from elsewhere "as if through a keyhole."[6] This Light was not the same as our conscience. In his *Apology* Robert Barclay wrote that "conscience, being that in man which ariseth from the natural faculties of man's soul, may be defiled and corrupted."[7] Early Friends believed our ability to follow the leadings of the Light is impaired, though not totally incapacitated, because of original sin. So "that of God in everyone" referred to our innate ability to respond to God, which we could attend to or ignore, something denied by the Calvinist Puritan culture of seventeenth-century England.

At the turn of the twentieth century, Quakerism in Britain shifted from a broadly evangelical community to a liberal one. Although these early liberal Friends wanted to reclaim the early Quaker vision, the meanings of particular Quaker phrases were altered. Liberal Quakers blurred the distinction between the Light and the conscience, rejecting the idea of original sin in favor of original goodness. The "inward Light" became the "inner Light," moving the Light to within the individual. Similarly, "that of God in everyone" morphed from our capacity to turn to the inward Light of Christ to a kind of divinization of the inner self.

Occasionally I've heard Quakers use the phrase "that of Good in everyone," presumably to include those with a non-theist outlook. In one sense I've no difficulty with this. If God is the greatest Good from whom all good things flow, then "that of God" and "that of Good" could mean the same thing. But I wonder if "that of Good" suggests there is only a part of us that is good. I believe, being part of God's good creation, that all of us is good.

The various ways "that of God in everyone" has been understood are important, but I have difficulty with "the Light" or "that of God" being seen as something identical with my own self. I'm wary of anything blurring the distinction between creation and God too much. I'm not God and God isn't me. I also don't like thinking of us each having a "piece" of God. I don't think God can be broken up into pieces. If we are to be united by "that of God in everyone" then God needs to remain whole.

I want to affirm the ability of everyone to respond to God, and the equality of worth of all people, but I don't want to sacrifice the distinction between God and humanity or the unity of God. I don't want to split God up or merge God and people. A helpful place to start is with Thomas Kelly's poetic understanding of "that of God within" in his book *A Testament of Devotion* (1941):

Deep within us all there is an amazing inner sanctuary of the soul, a holy place, a Divine Center, a speaking Voice, to which we may continuously return. Eternity is at our hearts, pressing upon our time-torn lives, warming us with intimations of an astounding destiny, calling us home unto Itself... It is a dynamic center, a creative Life that presses to birth within us. It is a Light Within which illumines the face of God and casts new shadows and new glories upon the face of men. It is a seed stirring to life if we do not choke it. It is the Shekinah of the soul, the Presence in the midst. Here is the Slumbering Christ, stirring to be awakened, to become the soul we clothe in earthly form and action. And He is within us all.[8]

16

Sometimes a helpful way to explain a metaphor is to use a collection of metaphors. I'd like to explore one particular metaphor, the "Shekinah," with the help of theologian Jürgen Moltmann and his book *The Spirit of Life* (1992). The Shekinah isn't a word found in the Hebrew Bible, but it was developed in later Rabbinic writings. In short, the Shekinah is the presence of God at a particular time and place, and the best way to approach it is through the story told about God in the Hebrew scriptures.

After the Hebrews escape from enslavement in Egypt, they find themselves wandering in the wilderness. God wanders with them, dwelling among them in a portable box called the Ark, which in turn lived in a big tent called the Tabernacle. Later, once the Israelites had settled in one place, they built a house for God, the Temple in Jerusalem, and God dwelt and rested there, specifically in the central room called the Holy of Holies. Then came disaster. The Temple was destroyed by the invading Babylonians and many Jews were taken into exile in Babylon. With God's house destroyed and God's people exiled, where was God to be found? This is where the idea of the Shekinah comes into play. God's Shekinah travels with God's people into exile, once more accompanying them in the wilderness, suffering with them and waiting to return home. Importantly, the Shekinah is not a piece of God. It's God's full presence. But at the same time, it's not God's omnipresence. It is God present at a particular time and place. The Shekinah is fully God and yet distinct from God. Moltmann calls this God's "self-distinction." God is both identified with God's-self, and with God's people. Through this self-distinction, God is present with us when we alienate ourselves from God. In the Shekinah, God is alienated from God. Moltmann writes: "This Shekinah does not leave us. Even in our most frightful errors, it accompanies us with its great yearning for God, its homesickness to be one with God."[9] It's a difficult, paradoxical concept, but one that, to me at least, makes poetic sense.

It's in this search for homecoming, for wholeness, that we can see the parallels between the Shekinah and "that of God in everyone." It's worth quoting Moltmann here at length:

> If we live entirely in the prayer 'Thy will be done', the Shekinah in us is united with God himself... It need not happen once and for all. It can also happen briefly, for a time... If we become one with ourselves, the Shekinah comes to rest... We become sensitive to the Shekinah in us, and equally sensitive to the Shekinah in other people and in all other creatures. We expect the mystical union of the Shekinah with God in every true encounter... We encounter every other created being in the expectation of meeting God. For we have discovered that in these other people and these other creatures God waits for our love, and for the homecoming of his Shekinah.[10]

Taking inspiration for the Shekinah, we can think of "that of God in everyone" as the indwelling of God in all creation. We are called to become sensitive to it and to answer it in ourselves and in others.

Chapter 5

Pray without Ceasing

Do you try to set aside times of quiet for openness to the Holy Spirit? All of us need to find a way into silence which allows us to deepen our awareness of the divine and to find the inward source of our strength. Seek to know an inward stillness, even amid the activities of daily life. Do you encourage in yourself and in others a habit of dependence on God's guidance for each day? Hold yourself and others in the Light, knowing that all are cherished by God.
Advices and Queries 3

The first two *Advices and Queries* spoke of God and the spirit of Christ. This third passage adds another word for the Divine mystery to our Quaker vocabulary: the Holy Spirit. It is to this Spirit that we are asked to be open, to be guided by. How are we to do this? We can be open to the Holy Spirit by setting aside times of quiet. Silence is a central Quaker tool for opening ourselves to the Spirit's guidance. Note how silence is not valued for its own sake. We don't worship the silence. This is not 'Silence' with a capital 'S'. The purpose of silence is to deepen our awareness of the divine and discover a source of strength in these depths.

There is no prescribed way to use times of quiet. There's no set time or posture and no suggested frequency. There's no prohibition against using song or movement or birdwatching to reach a place of stillness. All of us need to find a way into inward silence and openness, and we are free to find the way that works best for us. Remember that the aim is to deepen our awareness of the divine. This is the horizon we journey towards in all our spiritual practice.

The path of spiritual discipline is one of progress and growth. Can we cultivate through our spiritual practice a continuing and continuous sense of inward stillness? Can we, with Paul, rejoice always and pray without ceasing (1 Thessalonians 5.16-17)? Thomas Kelly found "those who have the gale of the Holy Spirit go forward even in sleep" (Qf&p 2.22). What begins as a simple suggestion to set aside times of quiet, becomes an exciting and terrifying challenge to live a life of ever-flowing prayer, of continuous connection to God. It suggests the life of the cloistered contemplative is available to us even in the hubbub of our daily lives.

Such a prayer-filled life is counter-cultural and can only come through practice and perseverance. Such a life is so challenging we can't do it by ourselves. We need encouragement from our fellow Friends and they in turn need us. We must support each other in this Quaker-style monasticism. Our spiritual lives are not private. We have a responsibility to each other for our collective spiritual health. Again we hear the message that we're not self-sufficient, we are not independent. We need each other and we are dependent on God. The guidance and strength we receive from God doesn't just come once a week. One hour on a Sunday listening to the promptings of love and truth in our hearts isn't enough. Like the Israelites in the desert, gathering manna from heaven (Exodus 16) and following the pillar of cloud and fire daily (Ex. 13.17-22), the Holy Spirit is present to feed us and lead us every day.

Not only are we to encourage each other outwardly in our spiritual discipleship, we are to hold ourselves and one another before God, in God's Light, inwardly in prayer. To hold another in the Light strengthens both the one who prays and the one who is prayed for. I firmly believe in the power of prayer. I also believe it's a great mystery. I don't understand it, but I don't think that's a good enough excuse for not doing it. If we live in a God-centered cosmos, then attending to God and lifting up our fellow creatures before God feels a very natural way to live.

With all this talk of spiritual discipline, we could fall into the trap of thinking our worthiness as Quakers depends on how spiritually disciplined we are. The final line of the passage protects against this. We don't undertake spiritual practices in order to earn the favor of God or our fellow Quakers. We do them because the Holy Spirit cherishes us and wants to bring us to new life. All are cherished by God, whether we set aside times of quiet or not.

Chapter 6

Wrestling with Jesus

The Religious Society of Friends is rooted in Christianity and has always found inspiration in the life and teachings of Jesus. How do you interpret your faith in the light of this heritage? How does Jesus speak to you today? Are you following Jesus' example of love in action? Are you learning from his life the reality and cost of obedience to God? How does his relationship with God challenge and inspire you? **Advices and Queries 4**

In Britain Yearly Meeting today you don't have to be a Christian to be a Quaker. The religious self-expression of individual Quakers takes many forms: Buddhist, Pagan, and Muslim, for example. In such a landscape of individual theological variety, what does it mean for the Religious Society of Friends to be rooted in Christianity? According to this passage, Christianity is not a chain to be cast off but the root structure feeding the Quaker tradition. To cut ourselves off from our roots might put the whole Quaker project in jeopardy. Whatever our own individual beliefs are, we cannot fully understand the Quaker tradition without understanding its Christian roots. So much of our common language, such as "Friends" and "the Light," is drawn from the Bible, particularly the Gospel of John. If we are to fully own our faith, then we have a responsibility to learn of its origins.

This responsibility is spelled out in terms of reflecting on the life and teachings of Jesus. Whatever our opinions of him, he can't be ignored. According to the passage above, the significance of Jesus is located in three areas: (1) His example of love in action. This is a man who fed the hungry, healed the sick, and emphasized how God is close to those on the margins; (2) His obedience to God. In living the prayer "not my will but yours be done" Jesus experienced estrangement from family and friends, made enemies of the religious authorities, and was executed by an occupying power; (3) His relationship with God. Jesus showed a startling intimacy with God, referring to God as "Abba" ("Dad"), and repeatedly withdrew from public life for times of private prayer. From Jesus we learn that to obey God is to live a life of love in action. To live such a life is costly and cannot be undertaken without a solid foundation in prayer.

In focusing on the "life and teachings of Jesus" many mainstream Christian understandings of Jesus are set aside. Here there's no Incarnation (the belief that Jesus is both wholly God and wholly human), no Resurrection (the belief that Jesus rose from the dead), no atonement (the belief that Jesus' death and resurrection reconciles God and creation) and no Second Coming (the belief that Jesus will return). There's no virgin birth and no empty tomb, no Jesus *Christ*. What we have is the Jesus of nineteenth-century Protestant liberalism, shorn of miracles and metaphysical claims. The Jesus of the *Advices and Queries* is a teacher and moral example, not a Savior or the Word Incarnate. This is a great shift from the first 250 years of Quaker belief in Britain and a break from the majority of Quakers around the world.

This raises many questions, particularly regarding our relationship with the Bible. This modern Quaker understanding of Jesus is markedly different from how the authors of the New Testament saw Jesus, for whom the Resurrection was of paramount importance. What are we to make of the New Testament authors? Do we distrust their motives? If we reject their account, upon what do we base our knowledge of Jesus? And how do we relate to our Quaker ancestors? When George Fox heard a voice say, "There is one, even Christ Jesus, that can speak to thy condition" (Qf&p 19.02), how are we to interpret it? How do we relate to our fellow Quakers across the globe, the overwhelming majority of whom trust the Biblical account? This *Advices and Queries* is a well-crafted, diplomatic passage. It affirms the importance of Jesus (if not Jesus' centrality) without making divisive theological claims. It does, however, raise questions we're yet to fully wrestle with.

I'm glad "challenge" and "inspiration" are paired together in this passage. Jesus is a figure of both mystery and hope. He is both frustrating and exciting. He refuses to be pinned down and summed up. His "otherness" is part of what makes him Jesus. Whatever we individually make of him, I hope he will continue to provoke the Quaker community to live ever more loving, risky, and prayerful lives of obedience to, in the words of Dante Alighieri, the "Love that moves the sun and the other stars."[11]

Chapter 7

A God Who Is Free

Take time to learn about other people's experiences of the Light. Remember the importance of the Bible, the writings of Friends and all writings which reveal the ways of God. As you learn from others, can you in turn give freely from what you have gained? While respecting the experiences and opinions of others, do not be afraid to say what you have found and what you value. Appreciate that doubt and questioning can also lead to spiritual growth and to a greater awareness of the Light that is in us all. **Advices and Queries 5**

How can we know anything about God? We can't have knowledge of God in the same way we have knowledge of objects. God doesn't have weight, height, color, or texture. God is not a *thing*. In the Bible, God is continually shown to be a hidden God with an unpronounceable name. So how can we have knowledge of such a Mystery?

According to this passage we have knowledge of God through experience of the Light. We can learn from the experiences of the living, but the dead should also have their say. The Bible, the writings of past Friends, all writings which reveal the ways of God, are lived experiences of God's Light. We cannot rely solely on our experience as an individual, which is fallible and limited. God is revealed to us through others, through a community extending backward through time. Neither should we discount our own experience, limited though it may be. Just as God is revealed to us through others, God is revealed to others through us. Knowing God is a collective project. Far from being a collection of individuals with private theologies, this passage exhorts us to be a community of robust theological debate.

We are asked to boldly speak about our discoveries and welcome doubts and questions. This passage reminds us that being a finder doesn't stop you from being a seeker. You can doubt and question without doubting and questioning everything. You're allowed some firm footing. To seek without the desire to find leads to aimless wandering and theological vagueness. To find and renounce further seeking leads to rigidity and self-righteousness. Seeking and finding go hand in hand. I find this tension of seeking and finding, of knowing and not-knowing, in the early Quaker understanding of how God is revealed through God's Word (John 1.1-5).

According to the New Testament, the Word (that which paradoxically God both is, and through which God creates and orders the cosmos) is not revealed through printed words on a page but is enfleshed in a living person, Jesus. God's Word is not an object or a tool, but a Life to be in relationship with. We can never know a person in the way we know a table or a chair. Can we ever say we fully know our closest friend? The first Quakers insisted that the Bible is not the Word of God. They experienced the Word of God as the living Christ present in their midst. Scripture, though of great importance, is words about the Word. As soon as we treat God's Word as printed words on a page, we are in danger of treating God as a thing we can know fully and therefore control.

The God revealed in the person of Jesus is totally free from any constraints we may try to impose. I originally wrote this chapter in the aftermath of an announcement that the US embassy was relocating to Jerusalem, a decision widely interpreted as a means to secure the votes of conservative evangelical Christians who believe such a move will hasten the Second Coming of Christ. This theology is based on an erroneous mid nineteenth-century interpretation of the Bible that treats it as the "Word of God" and suggests God's hand can be forced. If God is free, nothing we can do could possibly force God to act in any particular way. To put God to the test like this is, according to the Gospel of Luke, the theology of the devil (Luke 4.9-12).

So we are left with more questions. When we search for God as a community, and when we communally test our findings, is the freedom of God respected at every point? Can we hold the tension of seeking and finding, the tension of a God who is revealed in our inward beings and yet remains hidden? Such a project will, as the opening words of this passage tell us, take time.

Chapter 8

Learning to Disagree Well

Do you work gladly with other religious groups in the pursuit of common goals? While remaining faithful to Quaker insights, try to enter imaginatively into the life and witness of other communities of faith, creating together the bonds of friendship. **Advices and Queries 6**

What happens when we meet with difference? We might experience the excitement of learning something new. We might feel uncomfortable and alienated, especially if we find ourselves in a minority. We might be deeply disconcerted at having our values and beliefs, perhaps our entire worldview, challenged. To encounter difference is to have our sense of "normal" questioned, or to question the norms of others. How do we respond to the challenge of difference? The encounter with difference may be so challenging we seek to erase it. Difference might be experienced as a threat to the peace and stability of the group. "If we're not all the same, how can we possibly get along?" We might try and erase difference through coercion and violence, suppressing or destroying that which is different. A more subtle and perhaps unconscious way of erasing difference is to attempt to ignore it. I hear this in John Lennon's song "Imagine": if we could only forget about our religious and cultural differences, if we could forget our history, then we'd experience peace and unity. Like the words of "Imagine," are we, in the name of peace, guilty of treating difference as an illusion?

In *Advices and Queries* 5 we read about living in the tension of knowing and non-knowing. In the sixth I hear another tension, a tension between similarity and difference, acknowledging we have things in common with other religious traditions whilst recognizing there are Quaker distinctives. There are insights particular to Quakerism. The silence of Quaker worship is not a blank canvas waiting to be filled with other theologies. It's not a silence to be filled with the melodies of other traditions. The Quaker practice of silent worship is its own kind of music. It's our Quaker particularities that unite the Quaker community: the way we worship, the way we make decisions, the language we use, and the history we inherit. These are the materials we are given to treasure, celebrate, and work critically with.

Quakers should engage in dialogue with other traditions, and we should do so gladly. In such encounters we have the opportunity to grow in humility, to practice and receive hospitality, and to learn how limited our experience of the world is. God's ways are not our ways (Isaiah 55.8). God is "other" and in meeting with difference, we may hear the disrupting and renewing voice of God. We're also asked to remain faithful to Quaker insights. This acknowledges the possibility that, in encountering difference, we'll find our Quaker understandings challenged. It's a reminder that the purpose of inter-religious dialogue is not to reach a point where we're all in agreement. Disagreement and impasse must be expected. We may even have to state that certain beliefs or practices are incompatible with Quakerism.

Because dialogue is difficult and involves disagreement we need to enter imaginatively into the "other." Where are the differences as well as the similarities? Are there differences we're tempted to ignore because we find them too challenging? Such work takes patience and humility. Simplistic ideas that "all religions are the same" will not do. Other religious traditions are different. They have different ways of worship, different objects of worship, different understandings of "salvation," different histories, and so on. The bonds of friendship we seek are not based solely on how we are alike. Just as we must learn to love our enemies as well as our neighbors, we must learn to love in the midst of difference as well as similarity. The strongest bonds of friendship are forged in learning how to disagree well. The question, both within and without the Quaker community, is "how can we live in peace without erasing difference?"

Chapter 9

Expect the Unexpected

Be aware of the spirit of God at work in the ordinary activities and experience of your daily life. Spiritual learning continues throughout life, and often in unexpected ways. There is inspiration to be found all around us, in the natural world, in the sciences and arts, in our work and friendships, in our sorrows as well as in our joys. Are you open to new light, from whatever source it may come? Do you approach new ideas with discernment? **Advices and Queries 7**

My husband is a bird watcher, and over the decades of our marriage, I've been inducted into the ways of the birder, sitting in cold hides and waiting for an elusive bittern to emerge from the reeds, wandering heathland in the summer to the sound of a yellowhammer, or searching for orange-footed puffins hidden in a crowd of other cliff-nesters. When we hear a rumor of a rare bird sighting nearby, like a waxwing or ring-necked duck, how might I catch a glimpse of it? The bird watcher can acquire tools and knowledge and can become better with practice. Someone who follows the right social media feeds and has a good pair of binoculars is in a better position to spot a waxwing than I am. But however prepared, equipped, and disciplined we are, the birds remain entirely free. The bird watcher doesn't control the birds. So, it is with the Spirit of God at work in the world. We are called to be aware of it. This doesn't mean we can control it, possess it, or predict how it acts, but we can equip ourselves with practices and knowledge to heighten our awareness. We may seek God, but we never truly *find* God, as if God is hiding, waiting to be found. When we apparently find God, it's because God has chosen to reveal God's-self. God finds us.

God is so free, even freer than the birds, that when we put boundaries on the Spirit of God, God breaks through them. When it was thought God could only be encountered in special holy places, God surprised Moses by meeting him in the shrubbery of an ordinary hillside (Exodus 3). When God was thought to dwell in the inner sanctum of the Temple in Jerusalem, the thick curtain veiling the Holy of Holies was torn apart (Mark 15.38) and God was revealed executed outside the city walls. God is not only to be found in special places. God can be found in ordinary activities and daily experiences. God may meet us in the washing up or waiting for a bus, as well as in the Quaker meeting house. The God of the Christian story is unpredictable: "See, I am making all things new!" (Revelation 21.15, Isaiah 43.18). This is a God who will always act in ways we don't expect, for God's ways are not our ways (Is. 55.8). Therefore, spiritual learning must continue throughout life. As soon as we think we have God pinned down we must start all over again. God works not only within the Temple but beyond it. The curtain is torn in two, the banks of the river burst. Every aspect of our lives is a potential burning bush. All human endeavor can be illuminated with God's Light. There's not one moment where God may not meet us, surprise us, and make all things new.

The phrase most often quoted from this *Advices and Queries* is to be "open to new light." What does this mean? I have heard the expression that Quakerism is "rooted in Christianity, open to new light." This implies Quakerism is on an inevitable trajectory away from its Christian roots, and that Christianity is part of Quakerism's past and not its future. It also suggests that by "new light" we mean "other religious traditions." I believe the advice to be open to new light is not solely an invitation to seek beyond Christianity. Neither is it an instruction to endlessly seek without ever finding. Rather, at the heart of being open to new light is asking: "In what unexpected way is God going to act next?" To be open to new light is to expect the unexpected. God can meet us "in the natural world, in the sciences and arts, in our work and friendships, in our sorrows as well as in our joys." What other sources might God choose to act through?

But when the unexpected happens, how can you tell what is of God and what is not? When new ideas arise what commends them? Novelty alone is not enough. A new idea does not automatically mean new light. A new idea could be a deception, a distraction, a notion, and an idol. Does this new idea arise from the workings of the Spirit of God? This passage ends with words of fundamental importance. Our capacity to apprehend the will of God directly and accurately is impaired. We need to approach new ideas with discernment, which requires humbly bringing them before the community of faith. Discernment requires us to pay attention to what has gone before. Although God is free to act in new ways, we have stories of how God has acted in the past, and we have clues to God's character. The writers of the New Testament understood the Christ-event, a totally unexpected occurrence, by looking to the Hebrew Bible and showing how it retrospectively made sense. Likewise, the first Quakers believed the leadings of the Holy Spirit would never contradict the Bible. Our stories, tradition, and history are important tools for discerning whether a new idea is indeed new light. To be open to new light is not an individualistic, theological free-for-all. It's a recognition of the freedom of God to act in unexpected ways, and our own inability to know the will of God directly. Being open to a new light is a weighty yet delightful corporate responsibility. Where is the Spirit at work? What will it do next? How do we meet it together?

Part 2

Worshipping God

Chapter 10

Join the Thanksgiving of the Cosmos

Worship is our response to an awareness of God. We can worship alone, but when we join with others in expectant waiting we may discover a deeper sense of God's presence. We seek a gathered stillness in our meetings for worship so that all may feel the power of God's love drawing us together and leading us. **Advices and Queries 8**

The first seven *Advices and Queries* present a series of foundational theological principles, chiefly concerned with the nature of God and how we may know God's will. With the eighth, we begin the second group of *Advices and Queries*, which deal specifically with worship.

Worship is a response, rather than something we initiate. We don't make anything happen; something has already happened. God is God, and we can only respond with worship. Worship is about thanksgiving and giving thanks through sacrifice. Sacrifice isn't a payment. Abraham discovered this when God refused the sacrifice of Abraham's son Isaac. This God is not like the other Canaanite gods who demand the blood of children. Ultimately, not even the blood of animals is required: "The sacrifice acceptable to God is a broken spirit; a broken and contrite heart, O God, you will not despise" (Psalm 51.17). The prophets speak of the uselessness of blood sacrifice if it is not accompanied by justice: "For I desire steadfast love and not sacrifice, the knowledge of God rather than burnt offerings" (Hosea 6.6). Faithfulness, humility, love, and justice, this is how God wants us to give thanks, this is what makes our worship acceptable. These ideas come together in Paul's words to the

Church in Rome, which for me capture the essence of Quaker worship: "I appeal to you therefore, brothers and sisters, by the mercies of God, to present your bodies as a living sacrifice, holy and acceptable to God, which is your spiritual worship. Do not be conformed to this world, but be transformed by the renewing of your minds, so that you may discern what is the will of God — what is good and acceptable and perfect" (Romans 12.1-2).

Worship is something we do better together. We seek a gathered stillness, though not as an end in itself. We come together not for a quiet space or time out. The purpose of our gathered stillness is worship, and the purpose of our worship is to be drawn together (the binding ligaments, the *religare* of religion), and led by the power of God's love. Worship begins and ends in God's love.

How is it possible to worship alone? Perhaps it is possible because we are never really alone. Worship is an ancient song we join in with. It's a thunderous river we jump into. We add our pinch of incense to the aromatic clouds already billowing up before the throne of God. I have occasionally had the experience of being in worship with more people in the room than physical bodies. I believe we join in with the worship of all who give thanks at that moment. From the perspective of eternity, we also join all who have worshipped and all who will worship, the "great a cloud of witnesses" (Hebrews 12.1) known as the communion of the saints.

In my thanksgiving, I see myself in perspective. I remove myself from the center of things (what a burden to be at the center!) and take my place in the choir of worshippers. Not only must we remove our individual selves from the center of the universe, we must see the human race in perspective. If the God whose love we respond to is the Creator of all things, then it's not just humanity who is God's creature. Birds, trees, stones, seas, stars, angels, everything visible and invisible, conceivable and inconceivable, all created things give thanks to their Creator who loves them powerfully. We catch a glimpse of this in the Book of Revelation, where "every creature in heaven and on earth and under the earth and in the sea, and all that is in them" sings a song of praise to the Lamb (Revelation 5.11-14). Worship is our response to an awareness of God. To become aware of God is to give thanks for all that is Good, living renewed lives in response. To become aware of God is to become aware of our fellow creatures in all their vibrant mystery. To become aware of God is to find our rightful place in the cosmos, allowing ourselves to be led further and further into Love.

Chapter 11

Vibrant Silence

Every now and again I take part in a Quaker meeting for worship that is totally silent, a whole hour where not a word is spoken. To an outsider looking in, all such occasions may look the same, but to the worshipper, these experiences can vary wildly. Sometimes I leave worship with a sense of nourishment and have at times been graced with a renewed sense of connectedness to my Friends, God, and everything. I vividly remember one totally silent meeting where I felt a palpable, heavy presence of love in the room, and the glances, smiles and excited words I exchanged with fellow worshippers afterward confirmed this was a shared feeling. It was a truly gathered meeting. I have also experienced silent worship that was silent for a very different reason. These silences were dead.

Why are some silences vibrant, alive, feeling-full, and others dead and drab? Although the felt presence of God in a meeting for worship is ultimately a grace and not something we can control, I think the way we approach the silence is important. In many secular contexts, silence is a space to be filled. I have witnessed many meetings for worship where this attitude is apparent. The silence is a blank canvas for us to paint with our witty aphorisms and pious observations. This idea of silence only leaves us paddling in the shallows of God's ocean. The silence is not the space into which we speak, or even a space to think. Silence is a response to the Divine. Indeed, it may perhaps be the most perfect response. God dazzles Job with a sweeping poetic glimpse of the unfathomable mystery of creation, and Job can only respond "Behold, I am of small account; what shall I answer you? I lay my hand on my mouth" (Job 40.4). The Psalmist knows the limits of human knowledge when confronted with God's presence: "You hem me in, behind and before, and lay your hand upon me. Such knowledge is too wonderful for me; it is high; I cannot attain it" (Psalm 139.5-6). I have heard "ministry" in Quaker worship that is so wordy or intellectual as to be incomprehensible. We can struggle so hard to formulate our thoughts in worship that we miss the mystery altogether.

Silence is a response to mystery. I feel here that Quakers have an affinity with the sort of worship you might encounter in a Cathedral, as another response to mystery is music. C. S. Lewis in *The Screwtape Letters* imagines a Hell where there is only noise, with music and silence belonging to Heaven.[12] Silence and music are the most appropriate responses to mystery, acknowledging unknowing and the limitations of words. Silence is not a blank canvas, it's an offering. In worship, we offer our silence as we would offer a hymn or a dance. We might say the blank canvas idea of silence is *anesthetic*. It results in a numb, feeling-less space where nothing grows. Conversely silence as a response, as an offering, is *aesthetic*. It's a sensuous, feeling-full experience as one might have through the arts or sexual intimacy, with vocal ministry flowing from, and adding to its transformative power. I'm not saying we should expect mystical ecstasy every time we worship together. Deep silence can also be characterized by obedient listening, and there may often be times when God seems absent, protecting us from addiction to spiritual thrills as John of the Cross so wisely describes in his "Dark Night of the Soul."[13] However, in my experience, an anesthetic silence contains neither listening nor expectant waiting but is simply a void.

Does vibrancy in a Quaker community flow from the quality of worship or from the quality of everything else the Meeting does together? I'm becoming more and more convinced that vibrancy arises from relationship. God is love, so God is relationship. I rarely feel called to minister at a meeting where I'm a stranger and I think my lack of relationship with those present is part of that. The quality of our relationships with each other affects our communal worship. Jesus said "if you are offering your gift at the altar and there remember that your brother has something against you, leave your gift there before the altar and go. First, be reconciled to your brother, and then come and offer your gift" (Matthew 5.23-24). If we're experiencing "blank-canvas" meetings for worship week after week, we must examine our attitude to the silence and our relationships with each other. How often do we see each other outside of Sunday morning? How willing are we to give our time to eat together regularly? Do we know the joys and sorrows of each other's lives? We should not be satisfied with meeting for worship feeling continually like a dentist's waiting room.

Chapter 12

Offer Your Whole Self

In worship we enter with reverence into communion with God and respond to the promptings of the Holy Spirit. Come to meeting for worship with heart and mind prepared. Yield yourself and all your outward concerns to God's guidance so that you may find "the evil weakening in you and the good raised up. **Advices and Queries 9**

As someone with friends in many Christian denominations and with a heart for ecumenism, it's not unusual for me to attend worship where "communion" is synonymous with "bread and wine." If I'm not formally representing Quakers, I always take part. I believe in the unity of the Church, that Christ breaks all the boundaries we try to fix, and I see the ritual sharing of bread and wine as symbolic of that unity. The peace and connectedness I often experience after taking bread and wine communion is the same I experience in Quaker worship. The bread and wine may be absent but the spiritual communion is the same. In this way, Quakers celebrate communion with God. What does it mean to enter this shared communion with reverence? It means to enter with expectation. We go to worship with the anticipation that God might bind us together more strongly, and with a readiness to respond to the Holy Spirit. Reverence may sound serious and somber, but reverence can be deeply joyful. As C. S. Lewis said, joy is the serious business of Heaven.[14]

So, we come with anticipation and readiness. In reflecting on *Advices and Queries 8*, I wrote about the connection between worship and sacrifice. As well as coming with a sense of expectancy, we also bring our offering: a prepared heart and mind. Every day we have the opportunity to prepare our offering, to harvest a daily crop of gratitude, to confess an inevitable number of shortcomings, and hold ourselves and others in the Light. Then when we come together in our Quaker fellowship we can heap all this thankfulness, confession, and prayer onto the altar and see what the Holy Spirit makes of it. A wise Friend once said to me "If everyone comes to meeting empty, no one can go away full." We bring our spiritual bread and wine and feast together with God.

But we don't come expecting to get something in return. Our offering is not a payment or a bribe. In expecting God to do something, in anticipating the Spirit's promptings, we cannot then feel cheated if seemingly nothing happens. God doesn't owe us anything. We prepare our heart and mind not in order to receive an enjoyable worship experience each week, but in order to be more open to whatever God has prepared for us, which may be joy, tears, judgment, consolation, or apparently nothing. We prepare heart and mind during the week because one hour on a Sunday is not enough. If God is God, then worship is where we discover who we really are.

Yield! Relax and lay your burden down, for Christ's yoke is easy and Christ's burden is light. Yield! Put up your sword. Stop fighting. The struggle between God and creation is over. Remove yourself from the center. Christ is the Prince of Peace, not only outwardly between people and nations, but inwardly. The Holy Spirit brings peace to the inner war of our divided selves and weakens the power of evil. The only power evil has is from our power for good. A good word for evil is distortion, for evil is our good gifts used wrongly. The distorted good within us must be weakened through being healed and restored, through being put to the refining fire. As I write this, I hear the echoes of anti-LGBT+ Christian rhetoric, speaking of queer desire as a river that has burst its banks. It is unfortunate that "distortion" has these connotations because it captures how evil is not a thing in itself, but a distortion of God's good creation. Evil as distortion must not be thought of only in terms of sexual morality, as all our good gifts can be used wrongly. All our misdirected efforts can be realigned if we yield our whole selves to the guidance of God and the illuminating power of the Light.

Chapter 13

Talking About Evil

Quakers are often reluctant to talk about evil. Friends want to understand evil and see the good in the perpetrator, but they are often unwilling to condemn evil and are reluctant to see God as one who judges and rejects it. One of the contributors to the book *Twelve Quakers and Evil* (2006) writes "answering that of God in everyone means first of all finding it in, say, Fred West or Adolf Hitler."[15] But surely to say our priority is to understand the humanity of the tyrant is a slap in the face to those they are crushing underfoot. We need to be able to name the evil we witness and experience in the world, whether that's the evil of the suicide bomber or the evil of selling bombs to oppressive regimes. If we consider ourselves to be a community concerned with truth and peace, then we must call out lies and injustice. We also need to articulate the darkness within our own community. Without the language of sin and evil, we are ill-equipped to take the logs out of our own eyes (Matthew 7.3). For Quakers who believe in the goodness of humanity and the inevitability of moral progress, acknowledging the evil that Quakers have done and been complicit with, whether individually or as a group, is incredibly difficult. How can we affirm our experience of human goodness as well as the reality of evil and our responsibility for it? How can we hold these things in tension?

The "problem of evil," simply put, is how to square the belief in a good, powerful God with the existence of evil. Since the eighteenth century, attempts to solve the "problem of evil" have been known as "theodicies," a term coined by the German philosopher Gottfried Wilhelm Leibniz in 1710. Since then, evil has been explained variously as necessary for free will or the existence of good – how can we choose good if we can't also choose evil? – or as a way of making us better people, but any attempt at an explanation is problematic. If evil is explicable, if it has a reason to exist and is a necessary part of our world, then God as creator must be implicated in evil's existence. How can we worship a God who requires the possibility of the transatlantic slave trade or Auschwitz?

There's another perspective on evil that may be helpful for Friends. It's known by theologians as "evil as privation of the good," or as "privation theory." It affirms both the goodness of creation and our experience of evil without needing to explain evil as a necessity. Privation theory was developed in a Christian context by Augustine of Hippo, a fourth-century North African bishop and highly influential theologian.[16] In his youth he became a member of the Manichees, a religious group who believed the spiritual world was made by a good god and the material world by an evil god. Augustine later rejected their teachings, arguing that, from a Christian point of view, there was only one good God who created everything. Therefore everything, both material and spiritual, was good. So how did Augustine account for evil? Augustine developed an idea previously expressed by Ancient Greek philosophers that evil does not exist as a thing in itself. Evil is a corruption or lessening of good. It's an uncreated thing. Evil could be thought of as a hole in a sock. The hole is nothing in itself, it exists purely in relation to the sock. Take away the sock and the hole ceases to exist.

As evil doesn't exist, it can't be pursued for its own sake. When someone does something evil, at the heart of their action is the desire for something good. When the good that we desire is not the highest good (that is, when we turn away from God, from "that of God" within us) we commit evil. In 1961, philosopher Hannah Arendt reported on the trial of the Nazi bureaucrat Adolf Eichmann. In Eichmann, she saw, not a monster, but a very ordinary man. Eichmann pursued the goods of efficiency and hard work, and in doing so enabled one of the greatest atrocities of the twentieth century. Arendt coined the phrase "the banality of evil," capturing this sense that evil is committed not by especially evil people, but by those who are "terribly and terrifyingly normal."[17]

Privation theory also requires us to rethink our understanding of freedom. If freedom means freedom of choice, then only willing one thing (the highest good) sounds like imprisonment. But what if being free meant freely being our most true self? According to this understanding, our freedom increases the more we are what we were created to be. When learning to play the piano I had the choice to practice my scales or watch TV. I often chose the TV. But having that freedom of choice didn't make me freer to be a pianist. The more I practiced the more fluent I became. My freedom to be a pianist increased. Similarly, a virtuous person is not virtuous because they continuously choose not to do evil. To be freely virtuous is to not choose at all, but to be so practiced in virtue that good deeds flow naturally. The most freely virtuous person is the person who cannot help but be virtuous. From a privation theory perspective, freedom of choice was the "original sin." When Adam and Eve chose to trust the serpent, it wasn't that they made a wrong choice, it was that they thought there was a choice to make in the first place. The act of choosing was a turning away from a reliance on God, the highest good, to a reliance on their own will.[18]

So to put privation theory into Quaker-speak: (1) We are good in that we share in the goodness of God with all created things; (2) When we turn from the Light, from "that of God" within ourselves, our vision is darkened and our will weakened; (3) When we follow our corrupted desires, although they be for good things, we allow evil to flourish. We become less freely our true selves; (4) Only when we give over our own willing and desiring and "sink down to the seed which God sows in the heart" (Qf&p 26.70) will we find the evil weakening in us and the good raised up; (5) When faced with evil, we do not have to rationalize it as part of a Divine plan. Although good may come out of evil, evil is not required to bring about good.

To view evil in this way is both sobering and hopeful. All of us are capable of the most terrible evils, and we may be extending evil's reach in all manner of unseen and innocuous ways. Responsibility for the Shoah (the Holocaust) does not lie solely at the door of one dictator. Yet we can be confident that evil has no legitimate foothold in creation. God does not will it, require it, or excuse it. We are free to hate and reject it. Does this mean that we should destroy evil-doers? No, for every person is part of creation and therefore good. Evil is not a thing in itself and so cannot be destroyed. It's a hole in a garment that needs stitching, a corruption that can only be healed, and we are all in need of restoration.[19]

Chapter 14

Worship in the Desert

Come regularly to meeting for worship even when you are angry, depressed, tired or spiritually cold. In the silence ask for and accept the prayerful support of others joined with you in worship. Try to find a spiritual wholeness which encompasses suffering as well as thankfulness and joy. Prayer, springing from a deep place in the heart, may bring healing and unity as nothing else can. Let meeting for worship nourish your whole life. **Advices and Queries 10**

Worship is not always about celebration and fullness. Grief and emptiness have a role to play in the authentic faith community. Thomas Kelly writes that spiritual wholeness involves an enlarging of the heart, intensifying the joys and sorrows in our lives.[20] *Advices and Queries* 10 invites us to come to worship when we feel we have nothing to offer, realizing that our sadness, anger, tiredness, weakness, and desolation are in fact important offerings that our fellow Friends need. No meeting is complete without them. Our needs allow others to give. As well as asking in the silence, we can verbally ask trusted Friends for prayerful support. There is a real power in naming our needs. In the silence we can trust that the Holy Spirit is praying in us, for "the Spirit helps us in our weakness; for we do not know how to pray as we ought, but that very Spirit intercedes with sighs too deep for words" (Romans 8.26).

What if this time of spiritual coldness continues beyond one meeting? Do you still feel inspired to go to meeting, despite your inner emptiness? If so, then coming regularly to worship is a sign of faithfulness. To keep coming to meeting, even when we get nothing out of it, may be a time of important spiritual growth. It may be a wilderness time, a "dark night of the soul" that we will only truly understand once we are on the other side. It's important to share this journey with a trusted Friend, perhaps a spiritual director. Don't walk through the desert alone.

But there's another possibility. Sometimes, if we find ourselves in a long spell of spiritual dryness where going to meeting seems to make no difference, this might be a sign that something's not right. Maybe it's time to experiment, to try something else, or simply take a break. The key question is, are you going to meeting because you feel called to go in spite of the dryness, or are you going to meeting because that's what good Quakers do? If it's the latter, then maybe it's time to try not going to meeting. What love requires of you may sometimes be to stay at home. When I have done this, I've tried to do it with the blessing of my meeting, speaking to the people responsible for pastoral care and explaining my feelings. It's better that they know the reasons for such a decision, so they can offer support in the best way. "Accept the prayerful support of others."

Finally, *Advices and Queries* 10 also addresses the worshipping community, not just the individual within it. It reveals that true worship can take us in all our complexity. It can take our rage and our emptiness. Worship is not about playing a role. Worship should be somewhere where we can be our thoroughly disreputable true selves. This is a real challenge for the Quaker community. Can we hold each other in times of distress, where no easy answers are forthcoming?

Chapter 15

The Tightrope of Hope

Be honest with yourself. What unpalatable truths might you be evading? When you recognize your shortcomings, do not let that discourage you. In worship together we can find the assurance of God's love and the strength to go on with renewed courage.
Advices and Queries 11

The week in 2016 that US President Donald Trump arrived in the UK, I sat in worship with a deep sadness in my heart, weighed down by the moral cowardice of our political leaders. I felt so angry and powerless. As I offered these feelings to God, I felt my focus shift from the President to myself. It felt like I was being asked, "What have you done in response to the evil you are witnessing?" and I was unable to give an answer. I felt convicted of apathy, of not involving myself in politics at a local level. I can't remember the last time I wrote to my Member of Parliament. Was I entitled to feel so passionately angry about things that were happening at the top if I wasn't willing to engage at the grassroots level?

This is one of the primary functions of meeting for worship, this is when worship is truly apocalyptic in that the Light *reveals*. It shows us our true condition, which includes the bits we would rather remain covered up. God will not allow us to live in denial and delusion and, as long as we turn to the Light, it will show us how things really are, however unpalatable they may be. *Advices and Queries 1* also speaks of our "shortcomings." The New Testament uses the word *hamartia*, which means "missing the mark," and is traditionally translated as "sin." The Light shows us our sin, the way we fall short as individuals, as families, as communities, and as nations. I used to believe that thinking of myself as a sinner involved seeing myself as a disgusting worm; now acknowledging my sinfulness doesn't result in self-hatred. Such self-disgust would show me as captive to pride, invested in the illusion of my own moral perfection. Being a sinner is nothing special, and it doesn't erase our intrinsic goodness as God's good creation. We should be able to speak openly about our sin. Our meetings need to be "bullshit-free zones" where we can be honest about who we are. As long as we hold on to a need to be morally pure, as long as we are ashamed to be imperfect, we will hold ourselves back from the Light. Being honest means having the humility to open the closet door, allowing the Light to illuminate all that we wish remained hidden about our lives.

I said that God will not allow us to live in denial. Neither will God leave us to despair. The Light not only reveals our sin, it renews our courage to persevere. When we let go of reliance on our own strength, we can be filled with the strength of God. When we give up the need to be "good people," we can rest in the love of the Creator whose creation is fundamentally good. Out of the heart that trusts in God shall flow rivers of living, spiritual water (John 7.38), refreshing and rejuvenating. We may be able to find this spring alone, but the work is much easier when we undertake it together in a worshipping community.

In the committed life of faith, we walk the ledge between the chasms of denial and despair. This walk of vigilant hope is a difficult, wearying place to be, and requires a regular return to the Source to be reminded of God's love and renewed with God's strength. This is a way of tension, the tension of a tightrope: Jesus said, "my yoke is easy and my burden is light," and "if you would follow me you must take up your cross." The life of faith is both as simple, and as demanding, as turning to the Light within, facing what it shows you, and following where it leads.

The more power, wealth, and privilege we have, the harder our hearts will become and the harder it is to let in the Light. We shouldn't expect change from the hard-hearted leaders of the nations any time soon. We need to show them how it's done. In a world where those in power call evil good and good evil, putting darkness for light and light for darkness, and who are wise in their own sight (Isaiah 5.20), we are called to walk the narrow way of humility and hope, of serpentine-wisdom and dove-like innocence (Matthew 10.16), because with God's help we can do the work that needs doing.

Chapter 16

Building a Living Temple

When you are preoccupied and distracted in meeting let wayward and disturbing thoughts give way quietly to your awareness of God's presence among us and in the world. Receive the vocal ministry of others in a tender and creative spirit. Reach for the meaning deep within it, recognizing that even if it is not God's word for you, it may be so for others. Remember that we all share responsibility for the meeting for worship whether our ministry is in silence or through the spoken word. **Advices and Queries 12**

In entering worship, we don't seek a negation of the self. We seek to be full-filled, to have our horizon expanded beyond all that which preoccupies and distracts. God is both imminent, closer to us than our own breathing, and transcendent, above and beyond the individual and the human. God is among us and God is in the world. God does not want to blot us out, but for us to be fully ourselves, dwelling in God and God dwelling in us. We seek wholeness and the healing of our fragmented lives.

With this talk of healing and wholeness, some may ask what the difference is between Quaker worship and group therapy. Perhaps there is some overlap, but there are important differences. A meeting for worship is a public event and open to all, so anything spoken in worship is public testimony and not private confession. No automatic rule of confidentiality can be applied to what is shared in meeting for worship. There should be no taboo on discussing the content of vocal ministry after worship has finished. What we share in worship doesn't belong solely to us. If what we speak is truly ministry then it's God's word, a revelation of God, and God is not a private thing.

Being fallible, imperfect people, we don't always minister as we should. We may speak when we should be silent and be silent when we should speak. We might use the opportunity to speak in selfish ways. But God's word uttered through us in worship is never just for us alone, never just for our own healing or gain, so we need others to help us "test the spirits" (1 John 4.1). Did what we say come from the Holy Spirit, or from a spirit of pride? The worshipping community must wrestle with and digest the vocal ministry of its members, and not see these words as untouchable expressions of individual truth.

Of course, this wrestling should be done in a tender and creative spirit. We must lift each other up, not push each other down. In our meetings for worship for business, we are asked to conduct our decision-making in the spirit of worship. Conversely, we should also conduct our worship in the spirit of communal truth-seeking. Spoken ministry is part of our collective search for Truth. We are not casting our own individual pebbles into a pond, where the stones sink and remain untouched at the bottom, a collection of fragments. This image is too static and individualistic. We need an image that has direction, where these stones can form something coherent and unified, an image where there is a guiding Truth that gathers us together.

All ministry, vocal or otherwise, is service for others. Whatever gifts we possess are to be used for the building up of our neighbor and the community of faith. A helpful image for the shared project of our worship and ministry may be the "living temple" we read about in Ephesians 2.21. In offering vocal ministry we hope to be and become a living temple where God dwells. Quakers have a history of suspicion towards temples and other religious buildings. The first Friends called the churches of seventeenth-century England "steeple houses," pointing to the truth that the Church is a living community of people and not an inert building of stone. To think of the Church as a living temple is to see it as a dynamic, organic reality combining unity, interdependence, and growth. The Bible presents us with a living temple in its very first chapters – the Garden of Eden. This is a place where God is present and where humanity, God's image, has the priestly role of tending the garden. Quakers have long affirmed the "priesthood of all believers" (1 Peter 2.9). We are all called to be God's gardeners, nurturing the seed God plants in the human heart. In our wariness of "prepared ministry" (when someone speaks a pre-planned message that shows little attention to the movings of the Spirit) we might think vocal ministry should be completely spontaneous, a total surprise to the speaker as well as the hearer. It's true that vocal ministry can arrive in an unexpected way, but I've also experienced vocal ministry having a long gestation period. The seed of ministry will be sown in my daily life, during a conversation, whilst watching a film, or praying in private, but it may then take weeks before this seed sprouts and grows into a message I'm able to share during worship. When the message is ripe, I will only feel able to speak it in a community where ministry is received "in a tender and creative spirit." This is why the faithful keeping of a listening silence is also an important ministry. Through such listening we tend the soil of our worship, God's gardeners in the living temple, encouraging the spiritual seed to take root, flourish, and bear fruit.

Part 3

Being God's Witnesses

Chapter 17

My Whole Life as Testimony

George Fox's much-loved exhortation to "be patterns, be examples in all countries, places, islands, nations wherever you come,"[21] captures a key aspect of Quaker living, that we communicate our Quaker faith by our actions as much as our words. In the language of the Bible this is the idea that "faith without works is dead" (James 2.26). Quakers speak about this way of living as "testimony." Quakers today often talk about "the Testimonies," a list of values or ways of living. In Britain, this list is usually given as Simplicity, Truth, Equality, Peace, and Sustainability. In the USA, Quakers speak about Simplicity, Peace, Integrity, Community, and Equality. As well-loved as these values are, I have a strong dislike of "the Testimonies." I think they're too vague. Quakers don't have a monopoly on any of these values, and words like "peace" and "equality" can be interpreted in very different ways. I also think they're too specific. They can be treated like a pseudo-creed. I've heard newcomers to Quakerism say, "I don't think I could be a Quaker because I'm not a pacifist" or "I don't live a simple enough lifestyle to be a Friend." If we treat "the Testimonies" as privately held values, a menu to select from, boxes to fit our actions into, or a means of making us feel inadequate, then they're no longer a useful theological tool. In her book *Testimony* (2015), Rachel Muers writes that Quakers only started speaking of "the Testimonies" as a list of values relatively recently. They first appeared in print in the USA in 1943, and in Britain in 1987.[22] "The Testimonies" are not an immovable feature of the Quaker landscape. We don't have to use them if they no longer help us. There's another way we can think about this important aspect of Quakerism, and that is to see our whole life as testimony.

In the non-Quaker world, to give testimony is to speak publicly about what you've witnessed, about what you've seen, particularly in a court of law. What if we lived our whole life in the witness box? Then everything we said and did would testify to something, usually to what is most important to us. I think testifying is something we all do all of the time. Our words and actions tell other people what we value most, and what we think life is for. Once I'm conscious that my whole life is my testimony, once I realize that I'm in the witness box all the time, I have to ask myself what am I witness to? What is it I've witnessed? What have I experienced? The most important experience of my life is the never-ending love and grace of a God who is merciful and just. Every time I speak about that love, grace, mercy, and justice with my words or actions, I'm testifying to it. Living this sort of testimony is hard, and I don't think I'm very good at it. It's made even harder because many of the systems we live within aren't built on love, grace, mercy, and justice. Being a witness, and telling the truth, can make people who benefit from these systems uncomfortable or angry. Sometimes those people are Quakers. That's why I need to be part of a faith community. I can't be the witness I want to be by myself. I need other people to help me.

I testify to the love of God by living joyfully. As I've already mentioned in this book, I agree with C. S. Lewis that joy is the serious business of heaven. I love to laugh, dance, play games, eat, and drink, and take deep delight in living. Life is to be enjoyed and life has meaning. I testify to the love of God by living openly, proudly, and loudly as a gay man. I'm part of an LGBT+ running group, so part of my testimony involves running through the center of my home city covered in rainbows, witnessing to the wonderful existence of queer people. This is an important Truth, as not everyone is happy about us existing. As well as being openly gay in straight spaces, I'm openly religious in queer spaces. It's not unusual for me to experience the presence of God on the dance floor of a gay club, and I'm vocal about it. Being openly gay and openly religious challenges those who think the two are incompatible, and it's a witness to how the love of God is revealed in queer experience.

An important part of my testimony is being an openly imperfect person. I meet so many people who tell me they don't feel good enough. My reply is "I don't have it all sorted. I'm constantly failing to live a completely God-led life. But you know what, that doesn't stop God loving me, it doesn't stop God working through me, it doesn't make my feeble efforts meaningless." Part of living my whole life as testimony is letting the light shine on my darkness, it means looking at myself in all my messiness and failings and still seeing a beloved child of God. It means a commitment to keep following God in spite of my failings, and never seeing myself as unworthy to do so.

Chapter 18

The Quakerly Art of Squashing

How can we make the meeting a community in which each person is accepted and nurtured, and strangers are welcome? Seek to know one another in the things which are eternal, bear the burden of each other's failings and pray for one another. As we enter with tender sympathy into the joys and sorrows of each other's lives, ready to give help and to receive it, our meeting can be a channel for God's love and forgiveness. **Advices and Queries 18**

Have you experienced being squashed? I don't mean a "cozy" journey on the London Underground at rush hour, one of the few places you can have your head in someone's armpit for ten minutes without even a "hello." I mean, have you ever made a suggestion or had an idea that was, in the nicest possible way, roundly stamped on? In most Quaker communities there will be well-established members and, hopefully, newcomers. With age and experience comes power and authority. We can choose to use power wisely or abuse it. Unfortunately, we often abuse it unthinkingly with smiles on our faces. I have seen this happen in Quaker communities, with more seasoned Friends pulling younger or less experienced Quakers to heel.

I first discovered Christian theology through a course in Applied Christian Studies called "Workshop," led by the infectiously enthusiastic Noel Moules. The course left me bursting with ideas. There were so many things to chew over and discuss, and after each installment of the course, I returned to my local Quaker meeting with a fervor and thirst for religious depth. I must have been very annoying. Sadly, my memory is of being met by a wall of gentle disinterest. One particular conversation stands out. I suggested we could eat together as a community more regularly and an elder exclaimed "I couldn't possibly do more than I'm already doing!" Squashed!

At another Quaker meeting I attended, we had a very successful discussion about our shared ministry as a meeting. There was a strong desire from many Friends for greater visibility within the local community. My husband, during his brief and admirable attempt to join me in my Quakerism, suggested having an a-frame notice board outside the meeting house. No sooner had the meeting finished than an elderly and well-established member of the meeting came up to him, telling him very bluntly that no such thing was needed. People would find us when they were ready. Squashed! My husband held his ground well. He was under no illusion that the meeting was any less dysfunctional than his previous church, and he didn't let this brusque encounter deter him. How would a less-resilient person have responded? Would this have prevented them from making suggestions in the future?

One of the ideas that stayed with me from my learning with Noel is that the energy of a community comes from children and newcomers. The elders of the community are there not to control but to protect and nurture. Children and newcomers should not be patronized or humored, they should be listened to and encouraged. Of course, zeal and enthusiasm may yield unworkable or inappropriate ideas, but in my experience listening and tender questioning allow the individual to realize this for themselves. The quick "squash" may satisfy our desire for order and control, but it only leads to the stifling of the Spirit. Children and newcomers are not there to be controlled or molded in our own image. Age and experience can easily embitter us and sap our creative strength. Jesus says, "Behold, I am making all things new!" (Revelation 21.5). Creation is a key aspect of God. We are called to embody God's creative Spirit. Our job is not preservation but renewal. We are not curating a museum but messily making the artworks ourselves.

When children and newcomers offer their contributions, we can squash them with a gentle laugh, a pat on the head, and our agenda firmly holding sway. Or we can make the braver choice to receive them with a humble, wise, and listening heart, and the expectation of challenge and change.

Chapter 19

Why Don't Quakers Campaign on *X*?

I often see Quakers on social media expressing sadness that Quakers in Britain as a whole aren't at the forefront of campaigning for a particular cause, or against a particular problem. By not taking a collective stand on a moral issue the Quaker community falls short of their expectations. A source of this disappointment is the common belief among Friends that the natural place for Quakers to be is at the forefront of good causes. We like to think of ourselves as ahead of the curve on many social issues, as progressive, and generally on the right side of history. Although Quakers in Britain are a tiny community, we don't see this as an obstacle, instead thinking of ourselves as a group that "punches above our weight."

I wouldn't be surprised if this is rooted in the story we tell about Quaker involvement in the abolition movement.[23] Many individual Quakers were involved in anti-slavery campaigning, and over the last century you'll be able to find Friends involved in a wide variety of social justice movements. However, we tend to forget that it's rare for Quakers as a body to unite around any particular cause. An example of this is women's suffrage. Equality is a central Quaker value, and the spiritual equality of women was a foundational Quaker testimony. Because of this, we might naturally assume that Quakers would be at the forefront of campaigning for women's right to vote. But in 1910 and 1911, the London Yearly Meeting (as it was then called) was unable to agree a position on the issue.[24] Even when the Yearly Meeting makes commitments to action, however vague, convincing all individual Quakers that this applies to them is not straightforward. In 2021, Britain Yearly Meeting committed to being an anti-racist community. In February 2011, it agreed a national position to boycott products from Israeli settlements in the West Bank. How many local meetings and individual members of the Yearly Meeting realize these commitments apply to them?

The only hope that Quakers will corporately campaign for anything is if Spirit-led individuals campaign for a particular cause within their local Quaker community. The changing of hearts and minds is hard work. Rousing a whole community to action, and energizing a group of people to personally commit to a cause takes a lot of time and energy. This means only a very few of these campaigns (or "concerns" to use the Quaker term) will permeate the whole Yearly Meeting. Quakerism is set up to be a grassroots movement. If you're frustrated that Quakers aren't doing "x", then maybe that's the Spirit nudging you into this arduous, slow-burn work. We're a minuscule faith community with diverse social attitudes. There is very little we can all agree on. In recent years we have been unable to agree a position on assisted dying as a Yearly Meeting. Sometimes these differences go deep and are strongly emotionally charged, with conflicts between Quakers over gender diversity, population control, and vaccinations. Taking all of this into account, I think for Quakers to be at the front of any campaign would be a colossal achievement.

So perhaps this expectation of corporate political action comes from believing we are far more unified than we actually are. Although we celebrate diversity of belief, I often hear Quakers speak about the joy of belonging to a group of "like-minded" people. Despite our varied opinions, we are generally a monocultural group, much more so than other churches. Do those of us who represent this monoculture unconsciously expect to find Quaker unity in a sharing of White middle-class liberal values? I hope we can abandon our need for Quakers to be "like-minded," and instead seek spiritual unity across cultural difference. Early Quakers would often quote from

Ephesians, a book of the Bible that emphasizes unity. This unity is found in the Spirit (Ephesians 4.3). This Spirit, the Spirit of Christ, is a spirit of peace-making between different groups. Christ is described as breaking down the dividing wall of hostility between us (Eph. 2.14). For the first Christians, this wall was primarily between Jews and Gentiles (non-Jews), and the conflicts they had were cultural. If we're to remain faithful to this Spirit, we should expect our faith community to contain difference. Our experience of the Spirit doesn't erase these differences, making us all the same. Rather, the Spirit can unify us across and in the midst of our differences.[25]

After I enthusiastically joined Quakers in my late teens, I gradually learned that the Quaker community can't give me everything I need. I've had to let the ideal Quaker community in my imagination die. What I can expect of my Quaker community is that they will offer me a space to seek the energizing presence of the Spirit, take my experience of the Spirit seriously, and give me the support and tools to test what I think the Spirit is leading me to do. Fellow Quaker Martin Kelley said to me on social media: "I think at its best, Quakerism gives individuals non-judgmental community support to try something unproven, risky, or just a bit odd. Sometimes this slowly coalesces into a group norm but in the meantime, it's the building of individual leadings that starts change." What matters is if the work is Spirit-led, not that the work is labeled as "Quaker."

The expectation that Quakers should be active on all manner of social issues perhaps also comes from the idea that Quakerism is mainly about taking action, and building the kin-dom of God on earth. Of course, I think this quest for the kin-dom of God is hugely important. Jesus said it should be what we seek first and foremost. But I think we can emphasize Quakerism as action to the point where we forget that our worth as people is not tied up with the amount of good works we're engaged with. The language that expresses this best for me is that it's God who saves the world, not Quakers. The kin-dom we are seeking is God's kin-dom, which is ultimately of God's making. I don't think God can be collapsed into humanity. Yes, God calls us to this work, but this work isn't the foundation of our existence. In the creation story at the beginning of the Bible, God's finishing touch to the creation of everything is the Sabbath. The seventh day is not an afterthought. Seven is a number symbolic of wholeness. The Sabbath completes creation, it's the pinnacle of God's creative work. On this seventh day, God rests in creation and creation rests in God, and this rest completes us.[26]

Quakers say, "attend to what love requires of you, which may not be great busyness" (*Advices and Queries* 28). I would love to see us respond to this advice by cultivating a Sabbath spirituality. In the Sabbath, everything comes to a peaceful stillness of mutual enjoyment. We rightly value things for their usefulness but we also need to value things for their beauty, including ourselves and each other. In worship, we can be shown the brokenness of the world and be inspired to fix it, but worship is also about appreciating the beauty of creation. Quakers can rarely offer a unified political voice, but the Quaker community can and should offer a place to be with the Divine and be reminded that we are loved for who we are and not for what we do. Worship is about rest and the joy of being together as much as it is about seeking the kin-dom of God. Maybe resting in the "useless" beauty of holiness is as central to the kin-dom of God as our vital work for peace and justice.

Chapter 20

The Testimony Against "Times and Seasons"

One Easter Sunday, or "the day that is called Easter," to use an old Quaker way of speaking, I was worshipping with my Quaker community. Much of the vocal ministry referred to Easter and the Resurrection, with even the Archbishop of Canterbury's sermon getting a mention. This made me uncomfortable. Quakers don't have a Church calendar, at least officially, and have historically rejected designating any one day as more special than another. This has been called the "testimony against times and seasons." No Christmas, no Easter Sunday, and even the names of months and days rejected in favor of simple numbering. So, Easter Sunday, falling as it did on 17 April, could be "first day, seventeenth of the fourth month (the day the World calls Easter)." The way Easter Sunday seeped into our worship that morning felt to me like a forgetting of our Quaker identity.

What makes my discomfort strange is that I'm actually strongly drawn to the Christian liturgical year. As a Christian Quaker in a post-Christian community, I really appreciate being among people where the Jesus story is central. The liturgical year is an opportunity to rehearse and absorb the Jesus story, forming a Jesus-shaped community. I particularly love the theatrical nature of worship in cathedrals, having attended magical midnight masses at Christmas, and powerful Easter Sunday services full of candles, incense, and glorious music. Sitting in Quaker meeting for worship that morning, I thought "if I wanted an Easter service I could have gone to the Cathedral, and they'd have done it better."

This is fairly typical of my personality. I want to be all in or all out. Either we commit to a Quaker "plaining" of the year or cast off the plainness and revel in the smells and bells of ritual. A halfway house rarely works for me. But when I reflect on how I reacted to my fellow Friends' mention of Easter, I was being unfair. Quakers in the past may have had a "testimony against times and seasons," but this is no longer true in Britain today. Many Quaker meetings will have Christmas-themed worship in December. We have abandoned referring to Monday as "second day" and June as "sixth month," except in some formal documents like marriage certificates. In practice, the testimony has fallen away but nothing positive has replaced it. We find ourselves with no clear corporate answer on the place of times and seasons in the Quaker faith. If we take a look at why Quakers opposed times and seasons in the first place, we might be able to construct an approach that makes sense for us today.

When Quakerism emerged in the mid-seventeenth century, we can see four currents at work in the shaping of this testimony: (1) There was the desire to return to "primitive Christianity," to strip away all the idolatrous layers that had encrusted the Church over the centuries. This meant rejecting anything seen as nonbiblical or pagan, including Christmas celebrations and the names of days and months. (2) As well as looking backward, there was also a looking forward. Christ had come again inwardly in the experience of the Quakers, the future had arrived, and so any "meantime" festivals or rituals were no longer needed. Jesus didn't need to be remembered in bread and wine for he was present spiritually in the here and now. Christ's coming broke the circular time of the liturgical year, in a sense ending history. With Christ present inwardly, every time (as well as every space) was equally holy. (3) There was also a strong moral element to this testimony. Festivals like Christmas were seen to encourage drunkenness, excess, and immorality. Marking out Sunday as the Lord's Day was seen to encourage religious hypocrisy. The festivals of the Church meant nothing if they did not lead people to live more Christ-like lives. In this, early Friends were in harmony with the prophetic tradition of the Hebrew Bible, where festivals, fasts, and sacrifices are to be despised if they are not accompanied by justice (for example, Isaiah 58.6 and Amos 5.21-24). (4) By rejecting times and seasons, Quakers were visibly countercultural. By refusing to celebrate Christmas or by opening their businesses on Sundays, they marked themselves out as a peculiar people. Their behavior drew people's attention to the difference between the "shadow" and the "substance," which Paul speaks about in Colossians 2.16-17: "Therefore do not let anyone condemn you in matters of food and drink or of observing festivals, new moons, or sabbaths. These are only a shadow of what is to come, but the substance belongs to Christ."

Are Quakers today still attempting to return to primitive Christianity? Many Quakers still find inspiration in the life of Jesus, whilst disagreeing on whether he was purely human or the Son of God. The Jesus story is foundational for Quakers historically and globally. In a post-Christian society where Biblical knowledge is thin, it could be argued that a liturgical calendar is an important vehicle for communal storytelling. Perhaps adopting a form of liturgical year would help Quakers educate each other about their Christian roots. However, Quakers in Britain are post-Christian. Although there are individual Quakers who identify as Christian, and individual Quaker Meetings may have a strong Christian "flavor," "Christian" is no longer a label that can be applied to all Quakers in Britain. If the testimony against times and seasons has any practical function today, it's that it allows for a theologically diverse community. By not marking Christian festivals (at least officially) room is made for Quakers who find inspiration from outside Christianity, or who find Christianity to be unhelpful or harmful. The idea of rejecting pagan names of days and months no longer makes much sense, as there are Quakers today who also identify as pagans. The idea of returning to a primitive Christianity isn't as useful as Quakers once found it to be.

Does the Second Coming still play any role in Quaker theology? Do Quakers still experience the future as having arrived? Again, Quakers have diverse approaches to this. When speaking of the kin-dom of God, most Quakers will emphasize its presence in the here and now, although few identify this with the Second Coming of Christ. My belief is that, whilst I affirm the presence of Christ inwardly as the early Quakers did, I see Christ as "arriving" but not fully "arrived."[27] The fulfillment of Christ's arrival is still to come, as is evident from all the terrible, evil things that people continue to do to one another. I also think that the early Friends (and perhaps Quakers historically) haven't taken seriously enough the fact that we are creatures shaped by time and space. We exist in a particular location, molded by geography and culture. We age and change. As time-bound creatures, we live in a rhythm of ebb and flow. We are part of a wider community of creation. Our experience of life shifts with the seasons, as anyone with seasonal affective disorder will tell you. I find it much easier to commit to things for a season, like reading the New Testament during Lent, than doing the same thing every day. Perhaps the most common understanding of the testimony against times and seasons is that every day is equal, but I think we know this isn't really true. In my experience, some days and times are more special than others. Celtic Christianity speaks of "thin places," places that feel particularly spiritually potent. I think there are also "thin times," like wedding days and other celebrations and ceremonies. To say that all days are equal risks every day becoming dull and grey. A testimony against times and seasons that don't address the way we are creatures of time isn't a sustainable testimony.

Is there still a moral argument against times and seasons? Quakers are certainly not the first to suggest that festivities should be accompanied by justice. Almost every other church would agree with, say, keeping the spirit of Christmas all year round. It's possible to ethically celebrate and commemorate together. Although many Christians would agree the excessive consumption, waste, and expense of the Christmas season is immoral, most would not see this as an argument to stop celebrating Christmas altogether.

Is the testimony still countercultural? The claim that all days are equal is no longer shocking. The electric light bulb has freed us from the rhythm of sunrise and sunset. You can visit casinos in Las Vegas where time doesn't exist, restaurants, bars, and slot machines open 24 hours a day in windowless, brightly-lit halls. Trading on Sundays is no longer a remarkable thing, although in the UK Christian festivals still receive privileged treatment, from reduced trading hours on Sundays to public holidays on Christmas and Easter. When every day is a day to buy and sell, the testimony against times and seasons doesn't mark Quakers out in any useful way.

If the testimony against times and seasons doesn't make as much sense as it used to, we may want to officially abandon it, and formally recognize what is already happening: Quaker communities are free to celebrate whatever times and seasons they see fit. Another option is to reframe the testimony so that it becomes a useful part of the Quaker toolbox once more. I would find it helpful if our Quaker practice reflected the fact that we're creatures of times and seasons, fully part of the non-human creation rather than disembodied spirits. I would also find it helpful to be part of a storytelling community, where I can share with others the Jesus story that is fundamental to my faith. As we're now a post-Christian, theologically diverse community, we can't re-adopt the Church calendar, but we could communally acknowledge those points of the year that mark the changing seasons, the solstices, and equinoxes. These points can be meaningful to many people without attaching a specifically Christian interpretation. These natural way markers have the potential to be tent-like canopies under which we tell each other our stories. They could be containers for the different symbols we each hold dear, a way of sharing our beliefs without demanding doctrinal conformity.

This might sound like a complete abandoning or reversal of the testimony against times and seasons. If we see this testimony as purely a rejection of the liturgical year, then yes, it is. But the "negative" testimony of the Quakers (to use theologian Rachel Muers' phrase) always has a positive implication. By saying "no" to something we are saying "yes" to something else. By saying "no" to war, we are saying "yes" to a God of peace. By saying "no" to times and seasons, we are saying "yes" to a Spirit who cannot be contained by any special festival or building. "Now the Lord is the Spirit, and where the Spirit of the Lord is, there is freedom" (2 Corinthians 3.17). I see the Quaker rejection of bread and wine, holy water, special buildings, and Christmas as testifying to this Spirit of Freedom. Every day has the potential to be a time and place where God is revealed. The Spirit is free to be present where She wills, whether that's bread and wine or the silence of Quaker worship. The Spirit is free to break through any structures we might build to contain Her. We can keep this as a central Quaker understanding. There is nothing to stop us from witnessing the presence and work of the Spirit in unexpected times and places.

Seasons such as midsummer, Christmas, and Easter can be redeemed. They can be times of life-giving celebration that bring us closer to God and inspire us in our search for God's kin-dom. At the same time, times and seasons which are contrary to God's kin-dom can still be rejected. Celebrating some days doesn't mean celebrating all days. We are still called to "test the spirits to see whether they are from God" (1 John 4). In 2023 the UK "celebrated" the coronation of a new king. Is this sort of celebration consistent with our Quaker witness? In 2009 the UK began marking "Armed Forces Day." Although we no longer reject the names of days dedicated to the gods Odin (Wednesday) or Thor (Thursday), we can still reject a day dedicated to Mars the god of war, a day designed to cement the necessity and inevitability of armed conflict in our consciousness. We may even feel moved to witness against these days. One year on November 11, "Remembrance Sunday," I rejected the traditional two minutes' silence by leading two minutes of singing under an apple tree. I couldn't bear to take part in a ritual that, as I saw it, blessed violence as our savior.

So perhaps the best way to keep the testimony against times and seasons as a useful part of our Quaker toolkit is to keep it flexible. Quakers should not be a people who are hemmed in by dos and don'ts set in stone. If we follow the Spirit of Freedom, then we ourselves should embody that freedom. We are free to improvise as we go along, always guided by the rhythm of the Holy Spirit. When approaching any festival, if we ask "What helps nourish us as a people of the Light? What helps us bear witness to the reign of the Spirit of Freedom?" then we won't go far wrong.

Chapter 21

Bear Theology

At age 11, I learned that men don't kiss men. We were visiting an aunt and uncle, and I kissed my aunty when we were greeted at the door. As I moved to kiss my uncle, he stuck a hand out for me to shake. The gesture was very clear. I was too old to kiss other men now. Men don't kiss men. After decades of being openly gay, I look back on that moment and think "what a load of bullshit." But even so, this seemingly English taboo on men kissing men is hard to shake off. When you grow up in a culture that sees male displays of affection as shameful, the message gets deeply embedded in you.

Despite coming out in my late teens, it wasn't until my mid-30s that I began to feel part of a gay community. While out with gay friends, I was introduced to some other gay guys, and I instinctively stuck out a hand. The other man, who had been going in for a kiss, said jokingly "Oh, are we doing a manly handshake?" Of course, if I was the sort of person who prefers a handshake, then that would have been fine. But I'm not that sort of person. In that moment my own internalized homophobia became visible. Why shouldn't I greet another guy with a kiss?

In the corner of my home that I use for prayer, I have a picture of two bearded Jewish men kissing each other on the mouth with their arms around each other. It's a small, golden Eastern Orthodox icon from Israel/Palestine, given to me by a friend who knew instinctively that I'd like it. It represents the two leaders of the early Church, Peter and Paul, giving one another the "holy kiss" that is referred to in the New Testament (for example, Romans 16.16). By kissing one another, Peter and Paul symbolize the unity of the Church. Peter is the apostle to the Jews, and Paul is the apostle to the Gentiles (non-Jews). The inclusion of Gentiles within the early Church, which was originally a Jewish sect, was a source of great conflict, so this icon is a symbol of reconciliation.

I love the icon of the holy kiss, not only because it's a symbol of peace, but because, to my eyes, Peter and Paul clearly read as bears, and not the Winnie-the-Pooh kind. In gay culture "bears" are what we call beardy, burly, hairy, and cuddly gay guys, criteria which I more than adequately meet. I'm not claiming that Peter and Paul were gay, though some have, or lovers. That would be anachronistic, probably unlikely, and ultimately speculative. However, when I first saw the icon of the holy kiss, I couldn't help but read Peter and Paul in that way. In the straight world, I grew up in, men don't kiss men the way that Peter and Paul do. In the gay bear world, which I now get to be a part of, I see Peter and Paul everywhere. It's like they're the patron saints of bears.

In the company of bears, I see men express the joy of friendship through kissing each other on the cheek, on the mouth, hugging, squeezing, and caressing. Straight men might see this and assume such contact must be sexual, to which I'd say "yes and no." There's a sense in which such tactile male friendship is sexual. My favorite definition of "sexy" is "being comfortable in your own skin."[28] A key characteristic of bear culture is body positivity, a celebration of different shapes and sizes and all degrees of hairiness. You might say a central virtue of bear-ness is being comfortable in your own skin. So, the bear community is deeply sexy in a way that the straight world should be envious of: sexy, but not lascivious, sordid, or creepy. I can embrace and kiss my bear friends with no sense of infidelity to my husband. It's a mark of how screwed up a heteronormative world is when it assumes that kissing can only be between sexual partners.

The more time I spend in the company of body-loving bears, who are not afraid to express their friendship through physical affection, the more my internalized homophobia is chipped away. In a world where macho bullshit damages us all, bears model a "holy kiss" that expresses a particular kind of reconciliation, the reconciliation of men to their own perfectly imperfect bodies and emotions, and to their need for tactile male affection. Thank God for bears and the way they "greet one another with a holy kiss."

Chapter 22

A Quaker Theology of Trans Inclusion

When I first wrote this chapter in 2020,[29] a painful conflict centered on the inclusion of trans and non-binary people was rising to the surface within the British Quaker community. A big part of the conflict is where we start from. I heard some Quakers speak from a starting point of the safety of cis women, children, and lesbians. I want everyone to be safe and this is something all Quakers agree on, but this is an extremely problematic starting point as it treats trans and non-binary people (particularly trans women) as an inherent threat to the safety of others.

The Quaker tradition as practiced in Britain is built on the valuing of individual religious experience. It has always valued the inner life at least as much as the outward life. It involves trusting that when Friends share their inward lives, they are speaking the truth. The starting point for any discussion referring to trans Friends should be an affirmation and celebration of their identity, with cis Friends saying, "We believe you, you are who you say you are, and we love you." I'm then open to discussing, "So what implications does this have for *x*?" However, a starting point that implicitly says to trans Friends, "You are lying/deluded/wrong about who you are" and "you are a threat" undermines the theological bedrock of liberal Quakerism.

Thankfully, in 2021 Britain Yearly Meeting authoritatively stated: "With glad hearts we acknowledge and affirm the trans and gender diverse Friends in our Quaker communities, and express appreciation for the contribution and gifts that they bring to our meetings" (Minute 31).[30] Sadly, anti-trans sentiment in the wider public and political sphere has continued to intensify, and I still encounter Quakers who question the legitimacy of trans identities despite the Yearly Meeting Minute. This means thinking theologically about trans inclusion is very important. The future of Quakerism involves the full, affirming, and loving inclusion of trans and non-binary people or it doesn't have much of a future at all. I should add that it's not as if trans and non-binary Friends have yet to experience being included and loved by others in the Quaker community. Trans and non-binary Friends have been around for a long time. That the inclusion of trans Friends needs to be defended in the first place must be very painful for trans Friends.

I've already noted two things that go towards a Quaker theology of trans inclusion: 1) the valuing of that which is inwards at least as much as that which is outwards, and 2) the trusting of Friends to speak of their inward experiences truthfully. As a third, I'd add that in faithfully expressing who they know themselves to be, trans Friends enflesh the truth that a Spirit-led life leads to a reorientation, renewal, or discovery of identity. I was struck by the words of poet Jamie Hale in *the Friend* (27 September 2019): "The trans body is explicitly queer. It's visually different. It becomes a statement. It challenges the simplicity of sex categorization. You look at my body and there isn't really anywhere to put it." Jamie's comment made me think about the powerful testimony of simply being who you are, and how this testimony may be particularly visible in the lives of trans people. Trans Friends let their lives preach simply by being themselves. In the changing of names and the changing of bodies, they incarnate an important perspective on identity that can be found in both the Bible and the Quaker tradition, that who we are born as is not necessarily who we are or who we will be. (Of course, it's not incumbent upon trans people to be "explicitly queer." I wouldn't want to suggest that trans people who choose to keep their gender history private should do otherwise or have a less valuable testimony for doing so.)

Changing names is not so unusual. Many people change their surname after marriage, and I've known several couples who've chosen an entirely new surname to mark their partnership. I've known both cis and trans people who have changed their forename/s. In each case, a change of name says, "This new name better reflects who I am." This is something we see in the Bible too. In the Bible, a name is rarely arbitrarily given. A name describes who a person is. If a person's life changes significantly, their name might change too. After the death of her husband and sons, Naomi (whose name means "pleasant") chooses a new name, Mara (meaning "bitter") (Ruth 1.20). After Jacob wrestles with an angel, he is given the name Israel, meaning "the one who strives with God" (Genesis 32.28). Sarai and Abram, upon receiving God's promise to be the God of their offspring, are renamed Sarah and Abraham, Abraham meaning "ancestor of a multitude" (Gen. 17.5).

The name we are given at first may not be the right name for us in the long run. New experiences and new discoveries may prompt a change of name. There's a significant passage about names in the Book of Revelation: "Let anyone who has an ear listen to what the Spirit is saying to the churches. To everyone who conquers I will give some of the hidden manna, and I will give a white stone, and on the white stone is written a new name that no one knows except the one who receives it." (Revelation 2.17) This white stone is an invitation to the marriage supper of the Lamb, the great feast of all those who faithfully persevere through persecution for the sake of Jesus. This is saying that only when we are in intimate communion with God can we know ourselves fully. As we journey deeper with and into God, we continue to learn more about ourselves: "For now we see in a mirror, dimly, but then we will see face to face. Now I know only in part; then I will know fully, even as I have been fully known" (1 Corinthians 13.12).

As well as a change of name, the Jesus story points towards a change in our bodies, specifically at the resurrection of the dead. This is a mysterious (and perhaps embarrassing or absurd to liberal Quakers) aspect of the Jesus story and should be handled with care. I see it as an affirmation of the body. The body isn't something to be escaped. But it also points to some kind of future change, we are not what we will be: "Listen, I will tell you a mystery! We will not all die, but we will all be changed, in a moment, in the twinkling of an eye, at the last trumpet. For the trumpet will sound, and the dead will be raised imperishable, and we will be changed" (1 Cor. 15.51-53). This isn't about replacing one body with another. There is some kind of continuity. The resurrected Jesus is still recognized by his friends, although not initially. He still bears the wounds of the Crucifixion and yet he is also changed. The mystery of the Resurrection says that the future involves our bodies, and perhaps in a way we may not expect.

You may find this talk of a future resurrection hard to swallow. Thankfully, the first Quakers emphasized that such ideas about the future weren't to remain abstract. They believed that this hoped-for future was to be anticipated in the present. The way they were living, the intimacy with God they were experiencing, would one day be experienced by all. The marriage supper of the Lamb, the rebirth to new life in Christ, were things that could be tasted now. Early Quaker leader James Nayler referred to himself in his writings as "whose Name in the Flesh is 'James Nayler'" or "Written by one whom the world knows by the name of JAMES NAYLER."[31] He had inwardly received the white stone and knew that the name "James Nayler" did not capture who he now was.

In their journey of discovering who they really are, in faithfully living who they are on the inside and out, in being "explicitly queer," in their changing of names and bodies, trans Friends could be seen as enfleshing the journey cis people like me are also on. In incarnating the hoped-for future, they are inhabiting the important Quaker tradition of living the future now. So, I want to go beyond saying to my trans Friends, "I believe you, you are who you say you are, and I love you," and add "I thank God for your testimony. By simply being who you are God's glory is revealed and the Religious Society of Friends is blessed."

This chapter is a tiny contribution to a much greater effort. The changing of a name barely scratches the surface of what it means to be trans. There is much more to say, much more theologizing to be done, and as a cis man, I can only contribute so much. The best trans theology undoubtedly comes from trans people.

Few of us are who our parents expected us to be. All of us have much to learn about who we are. One day we will all see one another face to face, and I expect many of us will be surprised.

Chapter 23

Quaker Theology and Whiteness

The final chapter of this book represents a new stage in my theological journey. In 2022, I began researching Quaker theology and Whiteness as a PhD student. Questions of race and racism have returned to the agenda of Quakers in Britain in recent years, who committed to being an anti-racist community in 2021. I was able to be part of this conversation through my work at the Woodbrooke Quaker Study Centre, organizing national Quaker gatherings on diversity and inclusion in 2019 and 2020 with Edwina Peart, the Diversity and Inclusion Project Coordinator for Britain Yearly Meeting. A version of this chapter first appeared on jollyquaker.com in 2017, and I offer this as my early thoughts on Whiteness as a White Quaker.

It may be helpful to anticipate some questions other White Quakers may have. If Britain Yearly Meeting has committed to being an anti-racist community, why is this chapter on Whiteness and not anti-racism? To talk of Whiteness throws the spotlight onto White people and the system we are born into and perpetuate, in a way that talk of race or anti-racism doesn't. White people have a history of keeping race at a distance as if it doesn't apply to them. To give a seemingly innocuous example, I once competed in a rural flower show, where my homemade focaccia won a certificate of commendation in the category of "ethnic bread." Here, "ethnic" was taken to mean anything "non-British," and what counted as British was synonymous with a particular kind of White culture. I also entered some scones, but these weren't considered "ethnic." Like the scones, White British people like me don't think we have an ethnicity. To give a more serious example, when teaching in a White-majority suburb, I was told the school didn't have a problem with racism because it had only one Black student. The White students didn't have "race." Racism wasn't thought to exist in a room full of White people and instead was considered a Black or Brown problem. But the racism that Black and Brown people experience in Britain is created and occurs within a system of Whiteness. This system places a particular kind of pale-skinned European at the center of the universe, making them the measure against which all people are judged. Whiteness sets the standard for what is good, beautiful, and true. Whiteness determines who is important, who is worthy of attention, and whose needs have priority. Whiteness dictates whose stories we tell and how we tell them. To speak of Whiteness is to focus on the culture that creates racism, the culture that White people are shaped by and perpetuate. Where there are White people, however good their intentions, most likely racism will be found.

But what makes Whiteness a theological problem? Whiteness has a long history of entanglement with theology. White Christians have used theology to justify their persecution of Jews, their enslavement of Africans, and their colonization of indigenous peoples. Whiteness represents a profound distortion of how we understand God and God's creation. There are theologians today working to heal these distortions, examining what has gone wrong and offering possible solutions. White Quakers are beginning to wrestle with some of these problems, such as talking of "pastoral Friends" instead of "Overseers" with its slave plantation connotations, and asking how the Quaker theological metaphors of "light" and "darkness" sound in a culture that denigrates dark skin. A short chapter at the conclusion of a short book can only address a tiny part of this complex and wide-ranging work. Here I'm going to focus on how Whiteness operates through being invisible to those who benefit from it, how this invisibility needs to be dispelled, and how Quaker theology might help us in this work.

I'm just the sort of pale-skinned European that benefits from Whiteness, but for most of my life I've been completely unaware of this. Waking up to my Whiteness, and how I inherit and perpetuate it, has been a difficult experience. The slow process of illumination began in my late twenties when I was asked to speak at a local Anglican Church about Quakerism. After my talk, I opened the floor to questions. A Black woman in the congregation asked, "What about Quakers and slavery?" "An easy question," I thought, and launched into the story of Quaker abolitionists like John Woolman. This is the familiar tale Quakers tell about themselves, one of the foundations of their good reputation. Thinking I'd given an uncontentious answer, I was caught off guard when she angrily replied, "But Quakers benefited from slavery!" This wasn't part of the story I knew. I felt she was demanding I be ashamed of my Quaker identity. I felt exposed, became defensive and angry, and the conversation didn't end well. Of course, she was quite correct. Many Quakers did benefit from the enslavement of Black Africans, and individuals like John Woolman didn't represent the Quaker mainstream.[32] Quaker history is much messier than we would like it to be, but in that moment, my Quaker education hadn't equipped me for her question. I left the church that morning feeling wronged. I remained oblivious to my Whiteness, my White ignorance still intact.

The workings of my Whiteness in that instance were unveiled to me years later. In 2016 I was at Greenbelt, a liberal Christian arts festival, and attended an all-Black panel discussion. The speakers shared their experience of being Black in a society dominated by Whiteness. They shared how debilitating it was to be Black amongst White people who couldn't acknowledge the impact of racism, racism that they, as Black people, were aware of all the time. I suddenly understood why my answer to the question, "What about Quakers and slavery?" and my response to the anger it provoked was so naïve and harmful, so thoroughly White. I was part of the problem. My White ignorance prevented me from truly hearing what was being said. My unacknowledged Whiteness stopped me from stepping away from the center and humbly learning from another's experience.

Becoming aware of my Whiteness is a journey that's far from over. Whiteness is insidious, and learning about it leads into a tangled, deeply rooted thicket of thorns. It's an emotional journey and there's a strong temptation to remain focused on my own feelings, whether of anger or guilt, or despair at not being the good Quaker I thought I was. But White self-pity doesn't help anyone. If the journey is going to continue, I need to manage and move beyond these feelings. I've been helped to do this through re-engaging with a particular theological tool that Quakers have neglected: the language of sin. Quakers today rarely talk about sin, for reasons I explore in more depth in my book *Quaker Shaped Christianity*. I think this neglect of sin-talk puts us at a disadvantage when trying to understand the brokenness and inequalities of our world, including Whiteness. Quakers have a very positive self-image. It's easy for us to talk about sources of Quaker pride, like John Woolman, Elizabeth Fry or, more recently, the abolitionist Benjamin Lay. It's more difficult for us to talk about sources of Quaker shame, like the Quakers who profited from enslavement, or Daisy Douglass Barr who was both a Quaker minister and member of the Ku Klux Klan.[33] To help us handle and dismantle Whiteness without being paralyzed by guilt, I want to turn back to what in past centuries has been an incredibly influential statement of Quaker thought, Robert Barclay's *Apology* (1678).

To understand Barclay, we first need a little background information. I've heard it said that Quakers believe in original blessing, not original sin, but historically that's not quite true. In Genesis, the first book of the Bible, is the story of the first humans, Adam and Eve. They disobey God by eating the fruit of the Tree of Knowledge of good and evil. This first "falling short" has consequences for both Adam and Eve and their descendants, and so for the whole of humanity. This is the teaching called original sin. In the fourth century the North African bishop Augustine of Hippo said that, for the baptism of babies to make sense, every person inherits Adam's guilt. A baby is born with the guilt of Adam, is culpable for his crime, and so needs to be cleansed through baptism. This became the dominant understanding of original sin in the Western Church. Barclay says this isn't true. We are only guilty for the wrong things we personally do. We can't be guilty of another person's wrongdoing. However, although we don't inherit Adam's *guilt*, we do inherit Adam's *weakness*. As a result of Adam and Eve's disobedience (also called "the Fall") humanity became infected with a weakness of will, an inability to do good by our own strength. Barclay called this the "seed of the serpent."

The good news for Barclay is that there's another seed. This is the "seed of God" which God has planted in all people, the law of love that God has written on our hearts (Hebrews 10.16). God works on us inwardly through this seed. The seed is different to both our reason and our conscience, which Barclay sees as human faculties that can't lead us into Truth by themselves. Only when our reason and conscience are purified and illuminated by the light of God can they be reliable guides. (Barclay, like many Quakers at the time, uses the metaphors of seed and light interchangeably.) Barclay writes that we need to be liberated from the seed of the serpent and united with the seed of God. We can't do this by ourselves, and we may be oblivious to how deeply the seed of the serpent is embedded in us. The process of liberation begins when the seed of God cries out within us, asking us to allow it to grow. This growth can't happen without our permission, and it's a painful process. Because the seed of God is also the seed of Christ, we need to experience a spiritual, inward crucifixion and resurrection. Then Christ will live and bear fruit in us. The seed needs to break open before it can sprout. Even though we need to answer the cry of the seed, we can't choose the moment when this occurs. We must wait for what Barclay calls the "day of the Lord" or "day of visitation," but once the call of the seed is heard we can either receive God's seed or reject it. If we reject it, then our hearts may be hardened to the extent that we become unable to choose the seed again. If we refuse to open the door when we hear Christ knocking, the door may remain forever shut. Although Barclay is clear that it's the work of the historical Jesus Christ who makes our liberation possible, you don't need this knowledge of Jesus to experience the inward, spiritual crucifixion and resurrection. You can be united to the seed of God without knowledge of the Bible. You can know the mystery without knowing the history.

When we are united to the seed of God, Christ's work "roots out the evil seed," releasing us from the power of sin and clearing the way for the fruit of Christ to grow in us. Barclay describes this as entering a state of "perfection." Here perfection is not a static destination. The sort of perfection Barclay is talking about is a perfection of relationship, a dynamic way of being. There's always room to grow in goodness. Barclay writes that it's possible to turn away from this perfect relationship if we choose. Living in perfection requires hard work and perseverance. It's a journey.

The process of salvation Barclay describes matches my own experience of coming to terms with my Whiteness. The idea of the seed of the serpent as inherited weakness helps me make sense of what it means to be White. I inherit Whiteness through being born into a society that privileges certain people with pale skin, into a system of White supremacy. I shouldn't feel guilty about this. I don't inherit the guilt of White enslavers of the past. However, I do inherit the consequences of Whiteness and the many unconscious behaviors I have which keep Whiteness going. I'm caught in the long shadows of old sins. I'm entangled in the messy legacy of White supremacy, and I need to do my part in unpicking the knots.

I was oblivious to the legacy of Whiteness until I truly heard the voice of those "othered" by Whiteness and opened myself up to their experience. This "Day of the Lord," the moment when "the lights are turned on," filled me with distressing, complex emotions. Realizing my part in an oppressive system was painful, though it's a pain that dwindles to insignificance when compared with the pain of the Black Greenbelt panelists, or the Black congregant who had to bear the brunt of my ignorance about Quaker history. This realization was something I was never going to be "ready" for. If I had continued to refuse to listen to the experiences of the other, clinging to my self-image as a well-intentioned person untouched by racism, then the opportunity to see things from another point of view may have passed me by. As with Pharaoh (Exodus 4.21), the more privilege we have and the tighter our hold on it is, the harder our hearts can become.

I can know about Whiteness in a factual way, but this is also tough emotional work. It's heart-work as well as head-work. The history of Jesus is of a man seemingly crushed by a system of oppressive violence, but I remain unchanged by it unless I know the story inwardly. Having said that, the history is still of great significance. Knowing the history of White supremacy is vitally important if I'm to see how deep Whiteness goes. If Whiteness dictates what is worth remembering, then our work involves recalling everything Whiteness wants to forget. Maybe this is where we diverge from Barclay. We need to know the history even if we don't know the mystery. If the story that Quakers tell of themselves today is solely one of Quaker goodness, then it's a story distorted by Whiteness that needs correcting and retelling.

Like Barclay's description of perfection, once this work of "coming out" of Whiteness begins it's an ongoing process of liberation and transformation. Once you start to see systemic oppression you can't un-see it. I don't do this work to "help others" or in order to see myself as a "good person." This is about my own transformation and the transformation of other White people, in the hope of weakening the power of Whiteness. This is about entering into a continuing relationship of open, honest listening to the Holy Spirit speaking through Black and Brown voices, a relationship that requires continuous tenderness, pain, and humility, a continuous attendance to the God who is not White but is a refining fire that casts my Whiteness into ever sharper relief and may eventually burn it away (Malachi 3.2). Revisiting this chapter in 2023, I am reluctant to leave a tidy ending. Whiteness likes a neat conclusion and quick answers. I can already see the cracks in my theology and I end with these, expecting more cracks to be revealed as I take further steps on the journey: am I making Black pain a necessary component of my "Day of the Lord," as if God requires Black suffering for my own enlightenment? As Robert Barclay was a White man, does that make his *Apology* a highly inappropriate tool for understanding Whiteness?

About Mark Russ

Mark Russ is a writer, theologian, and teacher. Since 2013 Mark has written useful, Quaker-shaped Christian theology on his blog jollyquaker.com, and his work has appeared in *the Friend, Friends Quarterly* and *Quaker Studies*. His first book, *Quaker Shaped Christianity*, was published by Christian Alternative Books in 2022 as part of the "Quaker Quicks" series. His theological interests include hope, Whiteness, the roots of modern Quaker thought, and the theology of Jürgen Moltmann. Before retraining as a theologian, Mark enjoyed a successful decade as a music teacher in London, and spent a year visiting and living in various faith-based intentional communities in the UK and USA. He holds an MA in Music Education from the Institute of Education, and an MA in Systematic and Philosophical Theology from the University of Nottingham. From 2015 to 2022 he worked as a Programmes Coordinator at Woodbrooke, the international Quaker learning and research organization based in Britain. In 2022 he began a PhD at the University of Nottingham, researching modern Quaker theology and Whiteness. He lives with his husband in Birmingham, England.

Also by Mark Russ

Quaker Shaped Christianity: How the Jesus story and the Quaker way fit together

Telling the Jesus story through Quaker eyes; this is rich, readable theology that is both contemporary and rooted in tradition.

"What is Quakerism?" can be a difficult question to answer, especially when Quakers today struggle to find a shared religious language. In this book, Mark Russ answers this question from a personal perspective, telling his story of trying to make sense of Jesus within the Quaker community. Through this theological wrestling emerges a "Quaker Shaped Christianity" that is contemporary, open and rooted in tradition. In reflecting on how to approach the Bible, the challenges of Universalism, and the key events of the Jesus story, this book offers a creative, inspiring and readable theology for everyone who has wondered how Christianity and Quakerism fit together.

"The Quaker take on the Gospels is so refreshing because it's a thread of Christianity which has, sometimes, been bashful about expressing itself. *Quaker Shaped Christianity* offers an enjoyable combination of both simplicity and depth. The first-person guidance makes the book powerful but never solipsistic, and the author's tone is exactly as I like in my theological guides: forthright and gentle. I'm convinced it will really speak to many people who are on the courtyard of the sacred but are scared of their next step." **Tobias Jones**, journalist and bestselling author of books including *A Place of Refuge* and *Utopian Dreams*

A Message from the Author

Thank you for reading *The Spirit of Freedom*. I hope you've found it useful, thought provoking, and even inspiring. If you have a few moments, please write a review of the book on your favorite online site. This really helps extend the reach of the book. If you would like to engage further with my theological thought, please visit my website for an ever expanding range of blog posts, and news on my upcoming work: https://jollyquaker. com/.

In gratitude and friendship, Mark Russ.

Notes and References

Scripture quotations are from *New Revised Standard Version Bible: Anglicized Edition*, copyright © 1989, 1995 National Council of the Churches of Christ in the United States of America. Used by permission. All rights reserved worldwide.

Quotations from *Advices and Queries* and *Quaker Faith & Practice* are from *Quaker Faith & Practice: The Book of Christian Discipline of the Yearly Meeting of the Religious Society of Friends (Quakers) in Britain*. 5th ed., published by Britain Yearly Meeting, 2013.

1. Thomas Raymond Kelly, *A Testament of Devotion*, Reprint edition (San Francisco: HarperOne, 1941), 68.

2. This is from Margaret Benefiel's doctoral dissertation, referenced in Chuck Fager, 'Introduction', in *New Voices, New Light : Papers from the Quaker Theology Roundtable*, ed. Chuck Fager (Wallingford, Pennsylvania: The Issues Program of Pendle Hill, 1995), 4–5.

3. C. S. Lewis, 'On the Reading of Old Books', in *C. S. Lewis: Essay Collection and Other Short Pieces*, by C. S. Lewis, ed. Lesley Walmsley (London: HarperCollins, 2000), 442.

4. Gregory of Nyssa, *Gregory of Nyssa: The Life of Moses*, trans. Abraham J. Malherbe and Everett Ferguson, The Classics of Western Spirituality (New York: Paulist Press, 1978).

5. Stephen W. Angell, 'God, Christ, and the Light', in *The Oxford Handbook of Quaker Studies*, ed. Stephen W. Angell and Pink Dandelion (Oxford: Oxford University Press, 2013), 168.

6. Pink Dandelion, *An Introduction to Quakerism* (Cambridge: Cambridge University Press, 2007), 132.

7. Robert Barclay, *Apology for the True Christian Divinity* (Farmington, ME: Quaker Heritage Press, 2002), Prop V-VI §XVI.

8. Kelly, *A Testament of Devotion*, 3.

9. Jürgen Moltmann, *The Spirit of Life: A Universal Affirmation*, trans. Margaret Kohl (London: SCM Press, 1992), 50.

10. Moltmann, *The Spirit of Life*, 50–51.

11. These are the final words of Dante's epic fourteenth-century poem *The Divine Comedy*.

12. C. S. Lewis, *The Screwtape Letters: With Screwtape Proposes a Toast* (New York: HarperCollins, 2001), 119–20.

13. John of the Cross, *John of the Cross: Selected Writings*, ed. Kieran Kavanaugh, The Classics of Western Spirituality (New York: Paulist Press, 1987).

14. C. S. Lewis, 'Prayer: Letters to Malcolm', in *Selected Books* (London: HarperCollins, 2002), 283.

15. Quaker Quest, *Twelve Quakers and Evil* (United Kingdom: Quaker Quest, 2006).

16. G. R. Evans, *Augustine on Evil* (Cambridge: Cambridge University Press, 1990); William E. Mann, 'Augustine on Evil and Original Sin', in *The Cambridge Companion to Augustine*, ed. David Vincent Meconi and Eleonore Stump, 2nd ed. (Cambridge: Cambridge University Press, 2014), 98–107.

17. Hannah Arendt, *Eichmann in Jerusalem: A Report on the Banality of Evil* (New York, N.Y: Penguin Books, 2006), 276.

18. John Milbank, *Being Reconciled: Ontology and Pardon* (London; New York: Routledge, 2003), 8.

19. A shorter version of this chapter first appeared in 'The Friend' on 20 April 2017.

20. Thomas Kelly, *A Testament of Devotion*, 43.

21. George Fox, *The Journal of George Fox*, ed. John L. Nickalls (Philadelphia: Religious Society of Friends, 1997), 263.

22. Rachel Muers, *Testimony: Quakerism and Theological Ethics* (SCM Press, 2015).

23. Donna McDaniel and Vanessa Julye, *Fit for Freedom, Not for Friendship: Quakers, African Americans, and the Myth of Racial Justice* (Quaker Press of Friends General Conference, 2009).

24. Thomas C. Kennedy, *British Quakerism, 1860-1920: The Transformation of a Religious Community* (Oxford: Oxford University Press, 2001).

25. Willie James Jennings, *The Christian Imagination: Theology and the Origins of Race* (New Haven & London: Yale University Press, 2010).

26. Moltmann, *The Spirit of Life*, 276–96.

27. For more on the arrival of God, see my book *Quaker Shaped Christianity: How the Jesus story and the Quaker way fit together* (Christian Alternative, 2022).

28. Rob Bell, *Sex God: Exploring the Endless Connections between Sexuality and Spirituality* (Zondervan, 2007).

29. Many thanks to the trans Friends who gave feedback on the first draft of this chapter.

30. Minutes of the Yearly Meeting of the Religious Society of Friends (Quakers) In Britain At The Yearly Meeting Gathering Held Online, 19 July – 8 August 2021', August 2021. https://www.quaker.org.uk/ym/all-meetings/yearly-meeting-gathering-2021. Accessed 23 August 2023.

31. 'A Further Discovery of the Quakers'. Accessed 23 August 2023. http://www.qhpress.org/texts/nayler/further.html., and 'A Discovery of the Man of Sin'. Accessed 23 August 2023. http://www.qhpress.org/texts/nayler/manofsin.html.

32. For a greater exploration of this topic, see McDaniel and Julye, *Fit for Freedom, Not for Friendship*.

33. 'The Ku Klux Klan by Daisy Douglas Barr – Quaker Theology', 27 March 2020. https://quakertheology.org/kkk-daisy-douglas-barr/. Accessed 23 August 2023.

CHRISTIAN ALTERNATIVE
BOOKS

THE NEW OPEN SPACES

Throughout the two thousand years of Christian tradition
there have been, and still are, groups and individuals
that exist in the margins and upon the edge of faith. But
in Christianity's contrapuntal history it has often been
these outcasts and pioneers that have forged contemporary
orthodoxy out of former radicalism as belief evolves to engage
with and encompass the ever-changing social and scientific
realities. Real faith lies not in the comfortable certainties of
the Orthodox, but somewhere in a half-glimpsed hinterland
on the dirt track to Emmaus, where the Death of God meets
the Resurrection, where the supernatural Christ meets the
historical Jesus, and where the revolution liberates
both the oppressed and the oppressors.

Welcome to Christian Alternative... a space at the
edge where the light shines through.
If you have enjoyed this book, why not tell other readers
by posting a review on your preferred book site.

Recent bestsellers from Christian Alternative are:

Bread Not Stones
The Autobiography of An Eventful
Life Una Kroll
The spiritual autobiography of a truly remarkable
woman and a history of the struggle for ordination in the
Church of England.
Paperback: 978-1-78279-804-0 ebook: 978-1-78279-805-7

The Quaker Way
A Rediscovery
Rex Ambler
Although fairly well known, Quakerism is not well
understood. The purpose of this book is to explain how
Quakerism works as a spiritual practice.
Paperback: 978-1-78099-657-8 ebook: 978-1-78099-658-5

Blue Sky God
The Evolution of Science and Christianity
Don MacGregor
Quantum consciousness, morphic fields and blue-sky
thinking about God and Jesus the Christ.
Paperback: 978-1-84694-937-1 ebook: 978-1-84694-938-8

Celtic Wheel of the Year
Tess Ward
An original and inspiring selection of prayers combining
Christian and Celtic Pagan traditions, and interweaving
their calendars into a single pattern of prayer for
every morning and night of the year.
Paperback: 978-1-90504-795-6

Christian Atheist

Belonging without Believing

Brian Mountford

Christian Atheists don't believe in God but miss him:
especially the transcendent beauty of his music,
language, ethics, and community.

Paperback: 978-1-84694-439-0 ebook: 978-1-84694-929-6

Compassion Or Apocalypse?

A Comprehensible Guide to the Thoughts of
René Girard James Warren

How René Girard changes the way we think about
God and the Bible, and its relevance for our
apocalypse-threatened world.

Paperback: 978-1-78279-073-0 ebook: 978-1-78279-072-3

Diary Of A Gay Priest

The Tightrope Walker

Rev. Dr. Malcolm Johnson

Full of anecdotes and amusing stories, but the Church
is still a dangerous place for a gay priest.

Paperback: 978-1-78279-002-0 ebook: 978-1-78099-999-9

Readers of ebooks can buy or view any of these bestsellers by
clicking on the live link in the title. Most titles are published in
paperback and as an ebook. Paperbacks are available
in traditional bookshops. Both print and ebook
formats are available online.

Find more titles and sign up to our readers' newsletter at
www.collectiveinkbooks.com/christianity Follow us on
Facebook at https://www.facebook.com/ChristianAlternative